Living with a
Beagle

Edited by Sylvia Tutchener

BARRON'S

THE QUESTION OF GENDER
The pronoun "he" is used throughout this book instead of the impersonal "it,"
but no gender bias is intended.

ACKNOWLEDGMENTS
The publisher would like to thank Neill Hannon and the working section
of The Beagle Club.

First edition for the United States and Canada published
2005 by Barron's Educational Series, Inc.

© 2003 Ringpress Books

All inquiries should be addressed to:

Barron's Educational Series, Inc.
250 Wireless Boulevard
Hauppauge, NY 11788
http://www.barronseduc.com

International Standard Book Number 0-7641-5774-4

Library of Congress Catalog Card Number 2003115293

PRINTED IN CHINA THROUGH PRINTWORKS INT. LTD
9 8 7 6 5 4 3 2 1

CONTENTS

CHAPTER ONE

INTRODUCING THE BEAGLE

Happy, loyal, and with a face that can melt your heart, the Beagle is the most easily recognizable of breeds. His large, soft, brown eyes can cheer you when sad, and persuade you to forgive any of his mistakes (and there can be many!). Given his pleasant temperament, big personality, and small size, is it any wonder that he is such a popular pet around the world?

HOUND HISTORY

From the domestication of the wolf, around 14,000 years ago, humans have selectively bred dogs for various roles—as herders and drovers, as guards, as hunting partners, or simply as companions.

In the hunting category of dogs comes the hound, which can be split into two distinct groups—sighthounds (such as the Greyhound, Whippet, and Saluki), which rely on their eyes when hunting, and scenthounds (such as the Foxhound, Otterhound, and Beagle), which use their nose.

You can spot a scenthound a mile away. He has his head to the ground, and follows it with intense concentration, usually with his owner calling his dog back in exasperation—and in vain.

Physically, scenthounds are more heavily built than the lithe, athletic sighthounds, which rely on fast bursts of speed to catch their prey. Scenthounds require stamina to follow trails; they are muscular and strong, with well-sprung ribs to give them plenty of heart and lung capacity for their energetic work. The key feature is the hound's head. Scenthounds generally have long, pendulous ears, and, most important, a large nose, with broad, open nostrils. (See Chapter Seven, Seeking Perfection.)

Within the group of scenthounds, there is another division. Dogs were bred either for

Sighthounds, like this Greyhound, use their eyes when hunting.

Scenthounds, like this Beagle, rely on their amazing sense of smell.

large prey, such as deer, or for small prey, such as hare. The larger types (generally used for hunting deer) were known as Buckhounds, and the smaller ones Beagles.

MADE IN EUROPE

The exact origin of the Beagle isn't known, but it is likely to be European. Certainly, scenthounds were familiar to the Ancient Greeks. Around 450 B.C., the writer Xenophon referred to small dogs that hunted hare.

In England and Wales, recognized as the birthplace of the modern Beagle, small scenthounds were being worked before the Roman invasion (43 A.D.), and, by Arthurian times (500 A.D.), they had made the transition from being a dog used exclusively by the working class to catch a meal, to also being a hound used by nobles and royalty for the recreation of hunting. We know that the Prince of Wales, Pwyll, a contemporary of King Arthur, had packs of white hounds for such pursuits.

When William the Conqueror invaded Britain in 1066, he is thought to have brought the Talbot Hound with him. This was another white hound, now extinct, that was a very distant ancestor of the present-day Beagle, and that is also believed to have contributed to the Bloodhound.

BEAGLE BIRTH

The Middle Ages saw a distinct group of hounds:

- Northern Hound (fast and slender)
- Southern Hound (Greyhound-like build, with a long nose)
- Foxhound (large, for trailing deer)
- Beagles and Harrier types (smaller hounds, for hare-hunting).

Although Beagles are referred to in medieval times, they cannot be thought of as one uniform breed. The word "begle," found in English sporting publications, simply described the smaller scenthound breeds (see Name Enigma, page 13).

By the Elizabethan era (late 16th century), hunting was incredibly popular, and every nobleman of distinction had his own pack of hounds. Wire-haired Beagles were in existence, and some were small enough to be carried in the pocket. At this time, deer and hare were still the preferred prey, but by the mid-18th century, fox hunting was the favorite choice of many, and the longer-legged Foxhound was developed for this purpose (probably by crossing a Beagle type with a Buckhound).

By the turn of the 19th century, there were still many types of Beagles, including the Northern Beagle, Southern Beagle, and Cotswold Beagle. The wirehaired and smooth varieties were also in existence. There was still much interbreeding with different types, and Harriers and other types of hound were frequently introduced to Beagle lines. In fact, some people believe that the Beagle was created by a Harrier-Southern Hound combination.

DASH OF IRISH

The Kerry Beagle is also likely to have featured in the modern Beagle's makeup. Still around today, although without official Kennel Club recognition, this Irish breed goes back to the 18th century. Resembling miniature Bloodhounds, this black-and-tan dog is believed to have contributed its scenting ability to the Beagle.

Over the centuries, different hound breeds were developed to perform special tasks. The Basset Hound (left) is not as agile as the Beagle (right), but he is built to hold his nose close to the ground and follow a scent.

TERRIER TYPE

Some authorities claim that terrier blood was added to the Beagle in an effort to reduce his size. Small Hunt Terriers are likely candidates (and some have said that the Fox Terrier may have been added too), and this could account for the Beagle's tenacious spirit.

Exhibiting the Beagle in the show ring led to a uniformity of type.

CLASS BREED

While royalty and aristocracy turned their attention to fox hunting, the Beagle remained popular with ordinary people. Anyone could go "Beagling"—following the dog on foot—and Beagles could be kept inexpensively, without the need to maintain horse stables. With a pack of eager Beagles, the farmer and his family could always be sure of a meal.

The Pocket Beagle, popular in Elizabethan times, continued to be a hit with the upper classes, however. Less physically fit females, and children, would hunt with this small hound, which measured around 8 inches (20 cm) in height, while the more athletic family members took to the saddle, accompanied by their Foxhounds.

SAVED BY THE SHOW

The first Beagle was exhibited in the UK in August 1884, at the Tunbridge Wells Dog Society Show, and the Beagle Club of England was formed in 1890. This marked a turning point in the breed's history. Until then, the Beagle differed according to where it was bred; looks didn't matter too much—it was hunting ability that counted. If someone wanted a faster dog, or a better-nosed hound, he would add another breed entirely to the line. Coat type, size, and even shape were immaterial. With the establishment of the Beagle Club, the breed type was ready to be set.

At the end of the 19th century, hunting and shows were controlled by the Association of Masters of Harriers and Beagles, but its judges could not agree on the points to look for. So the first task of the Beagle Club was to draw up a scale of points, which was accepted by the Kennel Club as the Breed Standard, and that was very similar to the Beagle Standard used today.

WAR SETBACK

By the beginning of the 20th century, there was a consensus among breeders about what the Beagle should look like, although size was still variable. However, all the good work of committed breeders was about to fall apart.

World War I saw an end to dog shows, and most breeding programs came to an abrupt halt. Although shows were revived in the 1920s, Beagle numbers were small, and there was a desperate lack of quality breeding stock. The Beagle, together with a number of other breeds, faced a questionable future.

However, one woman, Nina Elms, came to the rescue. A breeder of Beagles, Basset Hounds, and Bloodhounds, Mrs. Elms' large Reynalton kennel kept the Beagle alive. Other breed devotees purchased stock from Mrs. Elms, and from there, Beagle numbers grew—only to be diminished again with the advent of war.

At the end of World War II in 1945, just one Beagle was registered with the Kennel Club. Fortunately, the Beagle is blessed with having dedicated, loyal fans, and, through the hard work of a small number of people (including Viscount Chelmsford, who reestablished the breed club), the Beagle began to recover—and eventually thrive—once more.

The Beagle has a big fan base in the United States.

AMERICAN HOUND

Beagles first set paw in America around 1640. Like their European counterparts, they were quite different from the Beagle we know and love today. Many resembled Dachshunds, though they were straighter-legged.

The dogs were particularly popular in the Southern states. However, the Civil War (1861–1865) put a stop to all hunting activities. When the war ended, in an effort to revive their stock, some breeders turned to England to import new bloodlines. General Rowett and Norman Elmore were two notable breeders who did just this in the 1870s, and interest in the Beagle started to grow.

In 1885, Blunder became the first Beagle to be registered in the American Kennel Club's Stud Book, and, soon after, in 1888, the National Beagle Club was founded. With this, and the first Breed Standard being drawn up by Rowett, Elmore, and a Dr. Twaddell, there followed a consistency of type, and the Beagle went from strength to strength, becoming a very popular show dog. At the Westminster Show of 1917, there were 75 Beagle entries!

POCKET SIZE

Small-size Beagles, so popular in Tudor and Elizabethan times, have persisted, and are still accepted in the United States, where there are two size categories for the show ring (see Chapter Seven, Seeking Perfection). Occasionally, undersized puppies are produced in the UK, which still make good companions, although they are not bred for show purposes.

With the first Breed Standard, consistency of type was established.

Although the Beagle is still used for hunting, his main role is as a loving and loyal family companion.

Beagling (hunting with a Beagle) became a popular pastime, and has been compared to the American equivalent of British fox hunting. This has almost certainly contributed to the breed's enormous success as a companion dog.

POPULAR PET

Although this dog is still used for hunting, his main role now is as a pet. Beautiful, with a low-maintenance coat, and a loyal, loving personality, it is not surprising that the Beagle is so well loved.

In the United States, the Beagle is the third most popular breed (after the Labrador and the Golden Retriever), with more than 45,000 registrations in 2003. Although the breed has never made quite the same impact in the UK, recently hovering around the 1,000 mark, the Beagle is still in the first five most popular hounds, and is a much-loved pet and a popular show dog.

NAME ENIGMA

- "Bée" is the French for "to stand open-mouthed" and "guele" means "mouth" (of an animal); when combined, they could refer to the breed's characteristic of baying when hunting
- "Beag" (Celtic), "begle" (Old English), and "beigh" (French) are all words for "small."

CHAPTER TWO

CHOOSING A BEAGLE

Even the most hard-hearted of people cannot fail to go weak at the knees when faced with a Beagle puppy. It's impossible to resist those large, gentle eyes, the soft, droopy ears, and the velvety puppy coat. Unfortunately, it's the breed's charms that are its downfall. Far too many people buy Beagles on impulse, without fully realizing what is involved, and then have to find another home for them when the novelty wears off.

To prevent future heartache, you must make sure that the Beagle is the right dog for you—and that you are the right owner for a Beagle.

Do you have the time for a Beagle?

Beagles are energetic dogs that require two walks a day, come rain or shine. You should also consider the time they need for training, which should be ongoing, to keep their minds occupied.

If you work full-time, a Beagle will be very miserable left alone all day; it is best suited to people who are at home all the time, or part-time workers. If your dog will be left for more than four hours, you should arrange for a dog-walker or friend to take him out to stretch his legs and alleviate his boredom.

Can you afford a Beagle?

On top of the initial cost for a puppy, there's all the equipment that you need to purchase (page 22), plus the ongoing costs of dog care, such as food, kennel, and veterinary bills. The latter can be very expensive if your dog develops a long-term condition. Pet insurance covers many treatments (depending on the policy) but not routine care, such as vaccinations or dental treatments.

Can you care for a Beagle for his entire life?

Your circumstances may be perfect for owning a dog now, but will they continue to be for the next 14 or so years?

You need to weigh all the pros and cons before taking the plunge into Beagle ownership.

Is your family as excited as you?

Everyone in the household should be consulted before you make a decision; after all, they have to live with the dog too. If someone is allergic to pets, it's important that they be tested with Beagles before you buy one. If you have children, ask yourself honestly if they are old enough—and well behaved enough—to have a dog (page 30).

Are you a doggie person?

If you are very house-proud or always like to look your best, a dog may not be a good idea, particularly one like the Beagle. Muddy pawprints on the kitchen floor, dog hair on your clothes, dog vomit in the car, and the occasional accident during house-training may cause you too much stress.

Is your home suitable?

Although, given the right exercise, Beagles can live in an apartment, a backyard is pretty essential during house-training, and it is preferable for them to have access to a safe outdoor area when they are adult too.

Can you cope with the noise?

Beagles are not normally vocal without reason, but some individuals can be rather fond of their own voice. It is wise to consider this, just in case your Beagle happens to be one of these. In many cases, it can be overcome with training (page 50), but some dogs are die-hard barkers or howlers. If this would drive you to distraction, choose another breed.

FINDING A BREEDER

If you are adamant that the Beagle is definitely the breed for you, the first step is to find a reputable breeder. Contact your national kennel club for details of breed clubs, and contact the secretaries for details of litters.

Visiting a dog show is another good way to go. There, you will be able to meet lots of Beagles, and can talk to people about what is really involved in sharing your life with one.

INTERVIEWING THE BREEDER

When you find a breeder that has a litter, do not rush in and buy a pup. When buying a car, would you pick the first one you saw for sale? A Beagle will probably be with you far longer than your car, so take your time to find the best breeder you can. Ask the following questions:

- How long has the breeder been involved with Beagles?
- Will the breeder take the dog back if you can no longer care for him?
- Will the breeder offer advice and support for the life of the dog?
- What are his or her reasons for breeding, and how many litters does he or she produce each year? (Are the breeders show people, who want a puppy for the continuation of their line, and for the improvement of the breed? Or are they in it purely for the money?)
- Ask about the litter's parents—why were those particular dogs used?
- Where will the litter be raised? A puppy reared in a loving, busy home will be used to all the sights and sounds of everyday life—the washing machine, vacuum cleaner, children coming and going, the telephone, etc. In a kennel, a puppy will not have this important start to life.
- If you have cats, finding a breeder who will raise the litter in the home where cats are present is important. The puppies will be used to the sights and sounds of cats, and will have seen that the adult dogs treat them with respect (see also page 33).

You need the space to exercise a Beagle—
or the time to take him for long walks.
Photo courtesy: Susan Arden.

It is important to see the mother with her puppies.

Watch the puppies play together, and you will see their individual personalities emerge.

Don't just take the breeder's word for it—ask around. Does the breeder have a good reputation for producing happy, healthy dogs? Ask other breeders at shows, and also seek the advice of breed clubs.

ASSESSING THE LITTER

When you've found the right breeder, you may have to be put on a waiting list until a litter becomes available. This is a good sign, showing that the breeder isn't churning out dogs like a production line, and that his or her puppies are in demand. When a litter is available, arrange to visit the puppies when they are around five or six weeks old.

- It's imperative that you meet the puppies' mother. She may be a little out of condition following the birth of the litter, but she will give you a good idea of how the puppies' temperament will turn out.
- Interestingly, the father of a litter, although he has nothing to do with raising the pups, also influences their character. If the stud dog lives close by, try to arrange to meet him. Careful breeders often require the "lines" of a stud dog many miles away, but a photograph may be available and the breeder should be able to vouch for the dog's temperament.
- Are the puppies reared in a clean, stimulating environment? The busier, the better!
- Are the puppies a healthy weight? The ribs should be felt, but not clearly seen. Avoid pot-bellied puppies (this may indicate worms).
- Do the puppies have clear eyes, and clean noses, ears, and bottoms?
- The coat should be clean and fresh-smelling. Part the fur, and look for scabs, or evidence of fleas or flea excrement (black specks).
- Are the puppies friendly and playful? Beagle puppies should be bold and full of life—never shy. If they are seen after eating, they may be lethargic; if so, arrange to visit them another time.

Resist the temptation of buying two puppies at the same time—you will have your work cut out for you looking after one!

TWO'S COMPANY

Beagles are pack animals and much prefer to live in a home where there is at least one other dog. If you already have a dog, that is great. If not, perhaps consider getting a second Beagle when your first puppy has matured to adulthood.

Do not be tempted to get two puppies at the same time, as siblings can develop a great rivalry with each other, and you will be so busy trying to cope with the mayhem of two puppies that you won't be able to give each one the individual care and training he needs. The two puppies are also more likely to bond with each other, rather than with you.

MALE OR FEMALE?

There are no differences, character-wise, between the sexes. Some people prefer the more masculine look of males, or the finer features of a female, but it is really a matter of personal choice.

If you are not going to neuter your Beagle (page 64), there will be practical considerations. A male is more likely to stray after females in season, and this, coupled with a breed that traditionally has a poor recall, can make life difficult. Your yard should be utterly escape-proof, and family members must be trained to always keep gates and doors shut to prevent the dog from getting out.

Intact (unneutered) females will come into season about every six months. During this time, your female will need to be kept away from all other dogs, or you could have an unwanted litter on your hands! She too will become quite clever and try to find a mate. Generally, female Beagles keep themselves quite clean during this time, but there can be some bloodstains to contend with, and possibly false pregnancies. Unless you plan to show your Beagle, neutering is by far the most sensible option, with many health benefits to commend it (pages 64–66).

BEAGLE COLORS

Tan and white.

Tri-color (tan, black, and white).

Lemon and white.

COLORS

The Beagle coat comes in any recognized hound color. Liver is not acceptable for the show ring. Tricolor (tan, white, and black) is the most common Beagle coat color, but tan and white is also popular. If you have a preference, you should let the breeder know, as this may limit your choice of puppy.

SHOW POTENTIAL

If you would like to show your Beagle, you should let the breeder know your plans before you purchase a puppy. A perfectly good pet Beagle won't necessarily make a successful show dog. He may not have the right markings, or the extrovert, show-off temperament, for example.

The breeder will assess the litter and will look for a Beagle that is a miniature version of the perfect adult, as described in the Breed Standard (see Chapter Seven).

However, bear in mind that a puppy showing promise at five or six weeks may not realize his potential. At this age, the tan color will only just be coming through. Or the dog may become too leggy, develop the wrong gait, or may just not like being the center of attention in the show ring. When you buy a puppy, there are no guarantees—and if he doesn't become a show dog, he will still make a wonderful companion.

If you plan to show your Beagle, you will need to assess conformation, coat markings, and movement, as well as temperament.

BREEDER PREROGATIVE

A conscientious breeder will be as fussy about finding the right homes for his or her beloved Beagles as you should be about finding the right breeder and puppy! Be prepared to be interrogated about your dog experience, lifestyle, home, and working arrangements. A good breeder will want to meet the entire family, including any children, and will be assessing you all the time to see if you fit the bill. Some will insist on a home check too. If the breeder doesn't seem interested in you, go elsewhere—he or she obviously doesn't have the puppies' true welfare at heart.

*The toys you choose must
be able to withstand the
rigors of chewing.*

PREPARING FOR YOUR PUPPY

Once you've found the perfect puppy for you, you may have to put down a deposit. Then it's a case of waiting until you can pick him up at the appropriate age (usually eight weeks of age, although it can vary among breeders). This can seem like an eternity, but there's plenty you should do to prepare for the new arrival, and to help the time pass more quickly!

Shopping

- Food (find out what the breeder is feeding the litter, and make sure you have the same brand/ingredients—see page 54).
- Crate (otherwise known as an indoor kennel, this can be fairly expensive, but is incredibly useful in the home and in the car, and will last for years).
- Bed/bedding (fleece bedding is soft, absorbent, machine washable, and quick to dry. If you don't use a crate, your Beagle will also need a bed; a hard, plastic one is tough,

easily cleaned, and can be made cozy with the right bedding).
- Collar and leash (some people like soft leather, but so do Beagles, who will try to chew it. A strong, nylon-webbing collar and leash set may be preferable).
- Toys (must be strong to withstand a puppy's chewing).
- Bowls (for food and water—stainless steel ones are chew- and break-proof).
- Grooming set (hound glove, guillotine-type nail clippers, canine toothbrush, and toothpaste).

Safety precautions

Never underestimate the amount of mischief that a Beagle puppy can get into! It's not just cats that are killed by curiosity, so make your home and yard as safe as you can to avoid any unnecessary trips to the veterinarian—and possible heartbreak.

- Get down on all fours and crawl around your

home. You'd be amazed at what you can see: trailing electrical wires, overhanging tablecloths or curtains within reach, cat food/litter tray, houseplants, etc. Treat your puppy like a toddler; if anything is dangerous or breakable, move it!

• Some popular house- and garden plants are poisonous to pets. Keep them out of reach, or change them for artificial ones! The Internet has lots of sites giving details on toxic plants (the American Society for the Prevention of Cruelty to Animals has a section on the American Poison Control Center, giving lists of dangerous and safe plants, as well as advice on making your home safe—www.aspca.org).

• Get organized! Persuade the entire family to be neat, putting shoes, toys, newspapers, cups, etc. away after use.

• Will the puppy be able to climb up to the windowsill? If so, rearrange your furniture, or be sure to keep windows closed when he arrives.

• Keep household cleaning materials, pet food, and medicines in a locked cupboard (toddler locks are ideal).

• Attach a basket around your mailbox to collect any mail. Otherwise the pup might get to important bills and documents before you do!

• Check your yard fencing. It must be at least 5 feet high (1.5 m), and there should be no gaps at the bottom. Gates must have a secure latch to ensure that they remain closed,

Beagle puppies are notoriously inquisitive, so you will need to check out the yard for potential hazards.

and everyone in the family must get into the habit of ensuring that gates are always shut behind them.

• Puppies can drown in swimming pools and garden ponds; use fencing to keep the puppy away, or, in the case of ponds, cover them with secure wire mesh so the puppy cannot fall in.

• Most accidents happen because the puppy isn't being supervised. If you are busy, and can't watch him, put him in his crate (see page 37) where he will be safe.

Finding a veterinarian

There should be a lot more to finding a veterinarian than just opening up the telephone directory and picking the first name you come across. Your Beagle puppy will be with you for many years, hopefully, and his health and well-being depend a great deal on the care of the veterinarian you choose. If you have a good, trusting relationship with the veterinarian, you are halfway there.

- Ask about what facilities are available at the clinic. Are there on-site blood-testing facilities, for example, or ultrasound scan machines?
- Are there any specialized departments? For example, does a qualified homoeopath or dermatologist visit the practice for referrals?
- Is the clinic within easy reach of your home? If you do not have your own car, is there good public transportation to it?
- Are the office hours convenient for you?
- What emergency-care provisions are there?
- Is the clinic clean, and is the staff friendly?
- Can your dog-owning friends recommend a clinic?

Visit several offices. Weigh the pros and cons of each before making your decision. And don't forget—you can always change to another if you aren't completely happy with the service.

Once you have found an office you are happy with, make an appointment for the day after you pick up your Beagle puppy. The veterinarian will give the puppy a health check, and discuss worming, flea control, vaccinations, microchipping, and neutering with you.

Choosing a name

Picking a name for your puppy should be fun— something that the whole family can get involved with. Here are some tips:

- Often, a puppy's character, habits, or appearance can produce some ideas. For example, a manic, energetic little puppy might be called Taz (after the cartoon character of the Tasmanian Devil).
- The puppy's kennel name may also give you some leads. For example, Finch's Nature at Harlington might be shortened to Harley.
- Choose a name that is easy to say; if it's too long, it will be impractical, and will only end up being shortened anyway.
- Remember that you'll have to live with the name for some years. Choosing the name of a pop star might appease the children for now, but will probably become outdated as fashions change!

PICKING UP YOUR PUPPY

Arrange to pick up the puppy in the morning, so you have the rest of the day to get to know each other before bedtime. Take along a helper, either to drive or to hold the puppy while you drive home. Make sure you take a form of payment, a bowl and some water (if the journey is a long one), and lots of paper towels for mopping up any accidents or sickness. The breeder will give you a receipt for the payment, and the pedigree/registration papers along with a copy of the sales contract.

Most breeders provide a little welcoming

package, with a diet sheet, some food, advice leaflets, details of the breed club, etc.

If you left a towel with the breeder as a comfort blanket for the puppy (see page 22), make sure you take it home with you; it might help the puppy to settle down on his first night away from his family.

Take written details of any veterinary treatments given to the puppy, such as worming (date, product, dosage).

RESCUED DOGS

Being such a popular breed in both the UK and the United States, the Beagle is a popular dog at the puppy farms (mills), where litter after litter is churned out with no consideration for the mothers or the puppies. The dogs are often in poor health and are not given crucial care or socialization. The puppies are usually sold to anyone who provides the money, with no consideration given to whether they are suitable owners. As a result, many end up in rescue.

Another chief cause of dogs needing another home is a change in the owner's circumstances, whether due to a new baby or divorce (with both partners having to move and to go to work, and therefore no longer able to look after a dog).

Fortunately, with love and patience, a Beagle soon adapts to a new home and family. The key is to match the dog to the owner. One dog, placed by Beagle Rescue in the UK, had home after home after home. Cooper, as he was called, was born with a great wanderlust, and his life was dedicated to escaping, chasing off after interesting smells, and then getting lost. After

At last the waiting is over, and it is time to pick up your puppy.

numerous homes, Cooper eventually found his paradise home—with a forester, who took the dog to work with him every day. With acres of forest to roam around in, Cooper's instincts could be satisfied, and he went home tired but content with his owner every evening.

If you are interested in giving a home to a rescued Beagle, your breed club will have details of welfare arrangements.

Sorrell Strange from Buckinghamshire, UK, and her partner, Stuart, both had family dogs as children, but, with two children of their own—Paige (ten years) and Millie (seven)—life was just too hectic to consider such a full-time pet—especially as Millie has special needs. However, since deciding to get a Beagle, the family hasn't looked back.

"When the children were younger, I really didn't have time for a dog," says Sorrell. "I was always off, taking Millie to physiotherapy and doctors' appointments, and it wouldn't have been fair. But, with Millie older, and both children now at school, we started to consider it as an option.

"Millie loves dogs—she would be a dog if she could! She lies down on the ground with them, and crawls on all fours when she sees one, which can be a problem if she encounters one in the street! Her behavior is much less erratic now too, and she isn't as aggressive as she was, so we started to look around.

"From the beginning, Stuart and I decided it had to be a Beagle. I had a Beagle-mix as a

After the first few nights, Ella quickly settled into her new home.

child, and my parents keep Beagles. They are the best-looking dogs—they are 'real' dogs, not too big or too small. I like their temperaments—and their great boldness. They can be little monkeys, which, with Millie, we're used to!

"We were also adamant that the dog had to be a rescue. There are far too many perfectly good dogs out there in need of a home, so I'd never buy a puppy. Plus, I don't have the time to run after a puppy. I'm busy enough as it is.

"We contacted a large animal rescue organization, but they weren't that happy with us, because Millie has special needs. In the end, we found the number for Beagle Welfare, and were impressed at how enthusiastic everyone was. Of course, there were concerns about our suitability, but a meeting was arranged for a couple of volunteers to do a home check, meet us, and introduce us to some Beagles. They wanted to see how the children reacted to the dogs, and vice versa.

"The meeting went very well. The assessors brought two Beagles with them that were crazy! They ran around, then raced out into the yard, sniffing every inch of it. Millie was astonished. She loved it, and rolled around with them on the floor. It was great—and we didn't want them to go!

"That evening, we heard that we'd passed the home check. The assessors believed an older dog would be more suitable for us, and, of course, it needed to have a superb temperament.

"Then it was just a case of waiting for the right dog to come along—and that dog was Ella. She was one of several dogs belonging to a breeder who died. She was very well loved, and had even been shown at Crufts. We went to meet her, and it was a match made in heaven. We took her home that same day, and both children were thrilled.

"We've had Ella for just over a month. We had a few problems for the first few nights. She was used to sleeping with other dogs, and didn't like having to spend the night downstairs alone. I slept with her a couple of times, and after that, it was like putting a baby to bed—we'd have to keep saying, 'It's okay, we're here' and then return to her after a few minutes, repeating that we were still there, and then gradually extending the time in between going to her again. Now, she's fine, and settles down well at night, though she's really excited to see us again in the morning, which is wonderful.

"The only other problem has been with the rabbits. With the male, Sweet Pea, Ella's fine. She gives him a sniff and a lick, and then leaves him alone. With the female, Kevin (named by the children, after their great-grandfather!), Ella just always wants to play with her. But Kevin isn't impressed, so we have to keep them apart.

"Apart from these minor things, Ella has been great. I think we have the best-behaved Beagle in the world! She doesn't chew the furniture or get into any mischief. I've even videoed her when I've gone out, to make sure she's okay— and she is!

"I would certainly recommend a Beagle to any other family with a special needs child. If Millie's noise gets too much for Ella, she just quietly takes herself off to her bed or to the top of the stairs. If Millie's arm waving gets too erratic, Ella disappears and comes back when it's calmed down.

"We've noticed a great improvement in Millie since Ella came along. Before, she had only a two-minute attention span. Now, Millie can watch a whole half-hour television program if she pets Ella by her side; she finds it very calming. It's great to see them together.

"Getting Ella is the best thing I've ever done. It's been a wonderful family experience. We all go for walks together on weekends—and we just can't imagine life without her now."

**Happy family:
Ella with Sorrell.**

CHAPTER THREE

ARRIVING HOME

After months of researching the right breed for you, and then finding the best breeder and the perfect puppy, you finally have your gorgeous Beagle puppy home. It can be rather daunting, if you have never owned a dog before; you might know all the theories about house-training, feeding, and so on, but the reality can be intimidating. You are responsible for keeping this little creature alive, and for making sure he grows up to be a happy, healthy, well-behaved, and well-adjusted adult. This book—and the advice of the breeder—will help you every step of the way. After a few days, caring for your puppy will be second nature, and it will soon feel as if you have owned him forever.

THE HOME

If you have children, and you have picked up the puppy from the breeder in the morning, you will be able to spend a few hours together, introducing him to his new home, before the little ones come home from school.

First take the puppy into the yard when you get home, as he will probably want to stretch his legs and relieve himself after the journey (see page 36, House-training). Then take him into one room in the house and let him have a good sniff around. If you have other pets, keep them separate for now, so the puppy doesn't have to cope with his new friends and investigating the environment all at one time.

Once he's had a good sniff around, cuddle him, give him some food (if a meal is due), and settle him into his crate for a nap (see page 37, Crate-training). All these new experiences are very tiring for a puppy that needs a lot of sleep, rather like a baby.

When he's confident in one room (such as the kitchen), maybe show him another (such as the living room). Have some toys on hand, to play together if the puppy is energetic. It's important that he realize that his new family are nice, fun people.

All interactions with young children should be supervised.

HUMAN FAMILY

Hopefully, by the time the rest of the family arrives home from work or school, your Beagle puppy will be feeling quite secure in his new home. Although children will be very excited to meet the puppy, it's important to keep excitement levels low; rushing in, screaming with glee, and roughhousing with the puppy is not the best way to start their new relationship together, and sets an unacceptable precedent.

It's important that children are given some basic guidelines from the start:

- The puppy should be picked up only if you are sitting on the ground. This prevents the puppy from being dropped and injured.
- There should be no indoor running/jumping around the puppy.
- Puppy toys are for the puppy, and children toys are for children!
- All toys, clothes, homework, shoes, books, etc. should be put away after use. If left within the puppy's reach and they get chewed, it's the owner of the property who is to blame, not the puppy!
- The puppy should always be treated gently. Rough-and-tumble games should be forbidden, as an excited puppy may bite in play, or could be injured by being trampled.
- The puppy is not a toy, to be picked up and played with whenever the mood takes the child. If the puppy is feeding or sleeping, he should be left in peace.
- Hands should be washed after petting or playing with the puppy.
- Sharing meals and snacks with a puppy encourages begging, and the food-obsessed Beagle will soon demand treats from your plate. If he's never given any, he won't expect them.
- Teasing, with food or toys, is cruel. Also, hitting the puppy if he does something wrong, is not acceptable. Teach the children to ignore the puppy if he jumps up, or is "naughty," and to praise the puppy when he is good. If the whole family is involved in the puppy's training, it helps with consistency—and is fun too!

A MOM TO MANY

When Jane May from Herefordshire, England had her first child, she was already an experienced mom to numerous dogs.

"I had seven Beagles when my daughter, Debrah, was born. We just took things slowly and gently, and the dogs accepted her right away. Debrah was especially fond of Bates and Angie, who were born around the same time as she. When she was two years old, Bates and Angie were a similar age, and she had an extraspecial relationship with them, as she'd grown up with them. The three of them would play silly games, share their toys, and roll around together, but they always respected each other.

"The older Beagles seemed to realize that they had to treat Debrah differently. They were very patient and gentle with her, understanding that, as a baby and toddler, she was a little clumsy.

"By the time Richard, my son, came along four years later, the dogs knew what was expected of them, and Richard quickly learned to respect them too.

"I'm a great believer in the crate, where a dog can have his own space, and escape for some peace and quiet. Both children were always taught to let the dogs be when they were having a catnap or just wanted some time alone.

"Beagles are a good breed for a home with children. They love people so much, and are gentle, sociable dogs. Plus, being canine vacuum cleaners, they enjoy being able to 'hoover up' after any crumbs or cookies that children drop!

"Debrah is now 18 years old, and Richard 14, and they have a great affinity with animals. Growing up with the dogs has taught them to be more patient and tolerant. Debrah is leaving for college soon, and I'm sure she'll miss the dogs more than she'll miss me!"

Debrah was brought up with Beagles.

When the children meet the puppy for the first time, sit them on the ground. Let the pup approach them in his own time (usually immediately!), and let him enjoy the fuss and attention.

Although the children may be anxious to get all their friends come to meet the new addition, it's important that the pup knows who his own family is before he meets everyone else. Have a "meet the puppy" socialization party in a few days, instead.

CANINE PALS

If you have an older, rescued Beagle that is well vaccinated, the introduction to your resident dog should take place on neutral territory, such as a park that neither dog is used to. Before placing a dog, most reputable rescue societies insist that the resident dog meet the prospective dog and that they get along, so the two should have met before and accepted each other.

- Walk the new dog in the park (on lead, as you cannot be sure of his recall obedience), and arrange for a family member or friend to turn up with the resident dog on lead.
- Let the two dogs sniff and say hello. It's important to keep their leads slack—a tight lead transmits tension to the dog.
- After an intitial sniff, continue your walk together.
- If there is any grumbling between the dogs, try to distract them, but don't be too concerned—they are just sorting out who's top dog, and will quickly come to an agreeable arrangement.

Beagles are pack animals, and enjoy being part of a larger canine family, so there should be few problems, particularly if you have a male/female combination. If you are concerned at any point, ask your veterinarian to refer you to an animal behaviorist.

When introducing a puppy, the introduction cannot take place in a public place, due to the health risk to the puppy (which is not yet fully vaccinated). Your yard will have to suffice.

Allow the adult dog and the puppy to get to know each other without too much interference.

MAKING FRIENDS

Dogs and cats can even become friends.
Photo courtesy: Susan Arden.

A Beagle can be amazingly tolerant. This Beagle, Miles, has learned to live alongside Degus, Doris, and Dizzy.

Although it is your resident dog's territory, he will probably be less protective of it than his own home.

The advantage of the backyard is that you can let both dogs off the lead, which will make them feel more relaxed. Many trainers recognize that an owner's nerves can be transmitted down the lead to the dog. Also, dogs are emboldened by having what they perceive as the backup of their owner, attached to them on the lead.

Although it's only natural to be protective of the little one, try not to interfere (unless the dog is in danger); the two of them will soon figure out how far they can go with each other. Also make sure there are no toys around during the initial meetings, as they could squabble over them.

Do make sure that you set time aside for your resident dog. A puppy is time-consuming, and it's easy to overlook your older dog in the early weeks, which could lead to jealousy. Enjoy your walks out together alone (the puppy will be too young), and make time for play and hugs.

FELINE FRIENDS

Beagles are hunting dogs, but, if they are raised with cats, most live quite happily with them. The importance of choosing a breeder with cats cannot be underestimated (page 17). If the first cat your puppy sees in his life is yours, he will be eager to play and will chase the poor creature. If he has been raised with cats for the first eight weeks of his life, they won't be especially interesting, and he will know, from having seen his mom's reaction, that they are not for hunting.

- Introduce the two animals in a closed room, but one where the cat can escape to the back of the sofa or a windowsill if she feels insecure.
- If the puppy shows an interest in the cat, distract him by calling his name. When he looks at you, give him a tasty treat. He'll soon realize that you are more interesting than the cat, and that it is worth his while to respond to you when you call.
- If the puppy gets too close for comfort, the cat will probably retreat to her "safe spot" and will observe him from a distance. Over time, his actions will be more familiar to her, and she will be bolder.
- Feed the cat on a raised work surface at first, so the puppy will not try to steal her food. You may have to continue to do this, although, once they are confident around the dog, most cats will defend their grub.
- It's also a good idea to keep the cat's litterbox out of reach—some puppies love to eat cat feces!
- Puppies can use the catflap to escape unnoticed into the yard, where they should be supervised. Either lock the flap, or bar access to it, until the puppy is too big to get through.
- If, over time, the puppy is still cat-obsessed, and you cannot trust him around her, consult a good trainer/behaviorist.

If you have a rescued Beagle, you should hopefully have ensured that he has lived happily with cats in the past. If his history isn't known, he should be cat-tested before you bring him home. Introductions follow the same principles as for the puppy, although extra care should be taken, as an adult Beagle is faster and more agile than a puppy. You might want to initially introduce the two by putting the adult in his crate and letting the cat observe the dog while he is safely incarcerated.

Stair gates are also useful for giving the cat a dog-free zone to which she can escape.

NAME CALLING

Having decided on the puppy's name before bringing him home (see page 24), you should teach it to the puppy from the very beginning. It's important that he associates only good experiences with his name; so, initially, don't use it to scold him.

- Sit the family on the floor in a large circle (or square, or triangle, depending on the size of your family), and arm everyone with a few treats.
- One person at a time should call the puppy's name, and ask him to come—*"Bertie, come!"* Said in an exciting, fun tone of voice, no puppy can resist obeying. As soon as he gets to the person, he should be given a treat.
- The next person should do the same thing.
- Make sure everyone sticks to the same name at first. Eventually, your Beagle will realize that "Bertie," "Bert," and "Bertram" all refer to him, but a young puppy may be confused. It will help him if everyone sticks to "Bertie."
- If this is repeated a couple of times a day, the puppy will soon realize that responding to this "Bertie" word is fun, and, over time, he will realize it is his own name.

FRIENDS NOT FOES

For Beagle breeders Linda and Deryck Player, the secret to multispecies harmony is to get puppies acquainted with cats when they are young. This usually instills a lifelong respect in the dog, although other people's cats are often exempt from his deference.

"We have always had dogs and cats together," says Deryck. "Our Beagles have grown up with having cats around, and so they just accept them. At the moment, we have Jill, a tortoiseshell-and-white cat, now 14 years old. She loves the dogs and will run up to greet them, rubbing herself against them.

PLAY ALL DAY

"We are breeders, and when we socialize the puppies and they meet Jill, all they want to do is play with her. There's no aggression there; they are just playful. Jill will sniff them and join in their games, rolling over to invite them to play.

"Other cats we've had in the past—Gareth, Gismo, and Sally—have just tolerated the dogs, as we rescued them as adults, so they had not grown up with dogs. Jill, on the other hand, has been with us since she was four weeks old.

TERRITORIAL ISSUES

"It's probably easier to introduce a kitten to a dog; it can be problematic to introduce a puppy to a household that already has an adult cat, as the dog is entering the independent cat's territory.

"It may take a little longer for them to settle together; the cat may show aggression or may disappear and hide somewhere, coming out only when the dog is not around. As time goes by, they should learn to become firm friends—or at least to tolerate each other.

"Kittens are more fascinating to a dog, as they are so 'flighty.' They move quickly and are more playful than older cats that may be more sedate. Whether you introduce a cat or a kitten, it's important to supervise them with the dogs, as it's in a Beagle's nature to chase something that moves quickly. Even our dogs, which are very used to Jill, will chase any 'strange' cats that come into our yard.

WATCH WORD

"Jill will go away if she finds it all too much; she might sit on the back of the chair or on the windowsill, and will watch the dogs with interest.

"Even after many years of having dogs and cats together, we always supervise them closely, in case play gets out of hand. The dog might otherwise become too excited, or the cat might harm the dog and scratch his face (possibly catching his eyes). You can never be too careful, and it's better to be safe than sorry."

Jill has learned that there is nothing to fear from Beagles.

Take your puppy into the backyard at regular intervals, and he will soon learn that he must be clean in the house.

- Say *"Bertie, come!"* before you give him his meals too, and before starting a game.
- This exercise helps with the puppy's recall too (page 45), which is essential for the errant Beagle.

HOUSE-TRAINING

Most puppies come with some house-training, as breeders usually start when the pups are around five weeks old. Even puppies that have had no formal introduction to house-training are still quite easy to teach, as all puppies are instinctively clean in their "nest," to prevent disease and to keep predators from detecting them through smell. The following house-

training program sounds simple, but, if it is followed religiously, it WILL work!

- Decide on a toileting area in your yard. A paved/patio area is easier to keep clean, but most puppies prefer grass.
- Take your Beagle puppy to this spot at the regular times—see box (opposite).
- At the toileting area, tell your puppy to relieve himself, using the same command every time (such as *"Be clean"* or *"Get busy"*).
- When he relieves himself, praise him effusively, and give him a treat. Then play a game in the yard together. Do not go right back indoors, or the puppy will associate relieving himself with the end of his fun time

outside, and will learn to hold on in order to earn some extra minutes in the yard!

- Stay with the pup until he "performs." If you leave him alone, you won't be able to train him. If it's raining, take an umbrella; if it's cold, bundle up!
- If, after 10 minutes, there's no sign of him obliging, take him indoors, be vigilant, and go outside again in half an hour (unless you see any warning signs in the meantime).

TOILETING TIMES

- As soon as he wakes up in the morning, or from a daytime nap.
- Before putting him to bed at night, or in his crate for daytime naps.
- After a meal.
- Immediately after a period of excitement (such as the arrival of a visitor).
- After play/exercise.
- Whenever you see the warning signs that he needs to relieve himself (he will circle and sniff the ground).
- Every two hours throughout the day.

- If the puppy has an accident in the house, don't shout at or punish him. He won't understand what he's done wrong, and will instead associate your anger with whatever he was doing at the time, such as playing. Instead, clean up the accident, and take him out more frequently.
- Even if you catch the puppy in the act, don't punish him. Just call him in a really excited tone of voice, smiling, and with arms outstretched, to encourage him to go out to the yard. The puppy should stop mid-flow, and follow. As soon as he finishes his business outside, reward him well and tell him what a good, smart dog he is. Punishing a dog for toileting will make him think that it's the act of relieving himself that makes you angry (he won't understand that it's the inappropriate location that displeases you). This could lead to him becoming more secretive in his toileting—hiding behind sofas to "go," etc.
- Don't become complacent. Even if your puppy is reliably clean in the house, continue to take him outside at frequent intervals. He is clean *because* you are taking him outside so often. Even seven-month-olds need reminding to "go."

CRATE-TRAINING

Before your Beagle puppy comes home, make the crate a cozy, welcoming place that he can call home. Cover the top and three sides (leaving the front open) with a blanket to make it draft-free and denlike. Then line the floor with newspaper, and put fleece bedding over half of it. This provides the puppy with bed and toilet areas (even with your house-training program, no young puppy can be expected to go through the night without relieving himself).

You can also place his food and water bowls inside. Feeding the puppy in his crate has many benefits; not only does it mean that he will associate his crate with the pleasant experience of eating (there are few greater pleasures for a

The puppy will consider the crate his own personal den.

Beagle!), but it will also mean that he can eat undisturbed, away from children or other distractions.

The chief advantage of the crate is that it is a safe place in which to keep the puppy for the short periods when he cannot be supervised (if you run errands for an hour), if you have contractors/workers in (who may leave doors or gates open), or while you bring the groceries inside. At night, a puppy can get into a lot of mischief (and danger), so a crate is a godsend.

Putting the puppy in his crate for short daytime naps, or to chew a safe toy for half an hour can prevent separation anxiety disorders. If you are with the puppy all the time, he can become overly dependent on you. This may lead to him becoming distressed if he is separated from you even for a few minutes. Prevention is far easier than cure!

Never use the crate as a prison, putting the puppy inside if he has been naughty. Nor should it be used as a dog-sitter, incarcerating the puppy while you go out to work for hours on end. If you work outside the home, you must arrange for a dog-sitter or a friend to look after your Beagle.

THE FIRST NIGHT

The first night that the puppy spends in his new home can be traumatic for him—and for you! This will be the first time that he has spent a night away from his mother and littermates, and he is likely to feel lost, even if he has settled well into his new home during the day.

- If the puppy needs to be fed before bedtime, take him outside to relieve himself after he eats.
- Settle him into the crate, ideally with a towel or blanket with the scent of his previous home (see page 22), say "Goodnight," switch off the lights, and leave the room.
- Putting a radio in the room, tuned to an all-night "talk" station may comfort him.
- Some trainers advocate keeping the crate in your bedroom initially, so you can talk to him to offer reassurance if he needs it. Others insist that the puppy should get used to his crate being in the kitchen (or wherever) from the beginning, and that if he starts off in your

It will take the puppy a few days to settle into his new home.

room, he will always want to sleep there. It's up to you to decide which approach to take.

• Experts are also divided on the crying issue. If your puppy cries in the night, some people believe you should reassure him and take him outside to toilet if necessary; others think the puppy should be left alone, believing that any intervention from you will teach the puppy to cry in order to summon you. Whichever approach you decide on, rest assured that all puppies learn to eventually settle down at night.

CHAPTER FOUR

EARLY LESSONS

The Beagle is a smart breed, but he is also terribly excited by life. If there is a squirrel to be chased, or a leaf to pounce on, he is quite likely to forget his training, preferring to investigate interesting smells and feel the wind in his face. Equally, if training sessions are long and boring, he will soon find his own amusement instead. The most important principle, then, is to make training fun.

Don't get too obsessed about accuracy, either. Although many Beagles have gone on to attain high levels of obedience (see Chapter Seven), where exercises must be performed with great precision, most people just want a fairly obedient pet that will sit, lie down, come, and walk well on the lead. If this is what you want from a pet too, who cares if your Beagle isn't sitting exactly straight? If you keep nagging him and repeating an exercise over and over and over, he will get bored and will be reluctant to involve himself in any additional training in the future. If his bottom goes on the floor when you say *"Sit,"* then he's fulfilled his side of the bargain, and deserves plenty of praise and a reward.

Training must be rewarding—and food is usually the way to a Beagle's heart.

Some puppies appreciate a game with a toy more than a food reward.

REWARD WANTED!

The days of making a dog comply with you in training are long gone. Old-fashioned methods of yanking a dog here and there with a choke chain and of barking out commands in a stern manner have been replaced with kinder—and more effective—ways of training. Where, in the past, dogs may have sat, rolled over, or walked to heel out of fear that they may be smacked or shouted at if they don't oblige, now they are being taught to WANT to work with you, making training more fun for them and you!

Persuading a dog that training is a rewarding experience requires... a reward! Would you go to work and give your best for no pay? If a bonus was up for grabs, would you work a little bit harder? Of course you would! The same applies to your Beagle.

For most Beagles, the ultimate reward is food. Use a selection of his favorite treats cut into small (but not miniscule) pieces that can be eaten easily. Cubes of hot dog, cheese, or baked liver are often popular. Initially, when first teaching a new exercise, use your Beagle's favorite, and give him a treat—and praise—when he does something you want him to do. When revising an exercise, you can use other enjoyable treats, but reserve his absolute favorite for when he needs to give that little bit extra.

If he does something wrong, don't punish him. Just ignore that behavior, and reward him when he does something good again.

THE MAGIC CLICKER

Clicker training is a very popular method of teaching dogs—and cats, and horses. The clicker itself is a small plastic box, which is held in the hand. When the tongue is pressed, it makes a distinctive "click" sound.

The trainer teaches the dog to associate the click

Puppies are easily distracted, so pick a training location where your puppy will be able to concentrate.

with a rewarding experience, done by clicking and then giving a treat. It takes only about 30 repetitions for the dog to understand that the click means a reward is coming. This is useful in a training exercise, as it means you can click at the precise moment that the dog does something good, but you can give the treat afterward, when he's finished that part of the exercise.

Dogs soon learn that they can control the clicks, that their actions may or may not result in a click (and then a treat). This makes them really think about what they are doing. If they don't hear a click when they do something, they will work hard to make it happen, and will offer another behavior instead. Once they've been clicked, they will offer that behavior again the next time, and, combined with verbal commands, will learn what is required for certain exercises.

Over time, you can click and treat less often. For example, once your Beagle has learned to sit on command, you wouldn't click and treat each time he did it, only if he responded particularly quickly, or every now and then to keep him interested.

There are several dog-clicker books on the market if you'd like to find out more, or you could join a training club that uses this method (many, many do, even for the basic puppy classes, so you are bound to find one nearby).

MOTIVATION

The exercises in this chapter can be used with a clicker, or you can use just praise and a food treat; it's up to you.

If you have a Beagle that isn't that excited about food as a reward, use a toy, or an ear tickle—whatever best motivates your particular dog. However, it is rare to find a Beagle that isn't a huge food enthusiast, so if your dog isn't enlivened by the treats you are offering, try other foods; it's likely that you will come up with something for which he will jump through hoops!

TIME AND PLACE

Learning something new takes concentration. If your Beagle is distracted by other dogs or people, by hunger, by tiredness, by needing to relieve himself, or by wanting to run around and let off steam, you won't get very far.

A treat can be used to lure the puppy into the **Sit.**

Initially, train indoors, or in your backyard, with only you and your dog around. This will help him to concentrate on you. As your Beagle masters each exercise, you can start to introduce distractions (such as another dog walking past, or some children playing with a ball at the end of the yard). Replicate any distractions you might encounter in the real world, a skateboarder racing past in the park, for instance.

SIT

- Hold a food treat in your hand, and make sure your Beagle knows it's in there.
- He will get excited, and will try to get it. This is good—by following the treat, he can be put in the right position.
- It takes a little practice to learn where exactly to hold your hand over the puppy's nose, but you'll get there in the end. Basically, you want it just above and behind his nose, so that he has to look up, and put his rump down, in order to reach it. Too high, and he'll go on his back legs, into a begging position; too low, and he'll go into a standing/crouching position.
- As soon as his bottom touches the ground, click and treat. Give lots of praise, and make a big fuss over the puppy, so he is left in no doubt that he has done something wonderful.
- Practice for a few minutes more, and try another five- or ten-minute session in a few hours. Little and often is the key to training, to reinforce the learning experience, but to avoid boredom.

- With practice, your Beagle will learn what position earns the magic click, and he'll get into position when you hold your hand above his nose.
- Then you can say *"Sit"* as he sits, so he can learn the command with the action. Again, with practice, he will understand what the word means. Once he does, he will sit on command.
- Ask the puppy to sit before he is given a meal, before you let him out of his crate in the car, before you put on his leash, and so on. Incorporating training into everyday life is useful for you, and keeps your Beagle's brain working.

DOWN

- The *Down* is performed in much the same way as the *Sit,* but you will need to hold the treat forward, in front of the puppy's head, and low to the ground.
- Make sure you have the treat in the middle of your closed fist, so that he can't sneak a bite, but he does need to know that it's in your hand.
- He will probably try to get it by keeping his bottom high, and stooping down with his front (in a play-bow position), but don't click and treat until his belly is on the ground.
- As soon as he's in the right position, click, treat, and praise him really well.
- As with the *Sit* exercise, practice little and often, then introduce the command *"Down."*
- With time, you can stop luring him with your hand, and he will go down on command.

You can apply a little gentle pressure to hold your puppy in the Down *so that he understands what is required.*

COME

This really is the most important exercise you can teach your Beagle. The breed is renowned for its poor recall, and many dogs are never let off the leash for fear that they will never come back. When he is older, you may be lucky enough to let your Beagle run free in safe, public places, but early, consistent training is a must.

All young puppies love following their owners around, and the Beagle is especially good at being a "shadow," as he loves people so much. As he gets older, he will become a little more independent, and will want to go off and

Start recall training as soon as your puppy arrives home.

explore on his own, so it's important to start training him to come while he is still naturally inclined to do so.

- Sit on the floor, indoors, with your puppy just a couple of yards/meters away.
- Call him to you, saying his name and *"Come!"* and use your most excited, fun tone of voice.
- Make your body language as inviting as possible. Stretch out your arms, and perhaps clap your hands to get him to you as quickly as possible.
- As soon as he comes, click and treat, give him a big hug, praise him profusely, and play a game together with his favorite toy.
- Practiced little and often, he will quickly understand that *"Puppy, Come!"* means there's some serious fun to be had—and he will want a piece of the action!
- When he's coming to you quickly from a short distance away, increase that distance a little. Then progress to calling him from

another room, and then calling him out to the yard, and then back into the house. Each time, be really happy to see him. You must make it worth his while to leave what he was doing and to come to you.

- Call *"Puppy, Come!"* when you put his meal down for him to eat. It may also help to reinforce this with a "toot-toot" of a whistle (use the same signal each time). This can come in useful when he may be out of calling distance in the future, and will help to save your vocal cords!
- The puppy's recall will be challenged outside, in the yard. You will have to compete with birds, squirrels, interesting smells, etc., so you will have to work especially hard to be the most interesting thing around. Carry some extraspecial treats/toys with you as rewards.
- Once your Beagle will come to you reliably in the yard, then stage some distractions. Ask a friend to sit on the grass and read a book,

Practice recalls in the yard, making sure you always have a reward to offer.

while you practice the exercise. If your Beagle still returns to you, then increase the stakes by introducing another dog.

- When you've succeeded in getting your Beagle back in your yard, despite distractions, you can try the exercise out in a park. Use a long training line. This is about 40 feet (12 m) long, and is attached to the puppy's collar. Unravel as much as you need, and then hold the excess. Initially, keep it fairly short, and, as your puppy comes back to you from shorter distances, it can be increased gradually.

- Be warned: Your Beagle may be perfectly obedient to the recall exercise in your backyard, but is likely to forget all his training elsewhere! Be patient—and never, never be cross with him if he is slow in coming back to you. If you shout at him, he'll be even more reluctant to oblige in the future.

- When the puppy is sniffing around (still on the leash) and playing, call him every now and then, click him, and give him one of the treats you reserve for extraspecial occasions. Then send him off to play again. Never call him back to just put his normal leash on and to take him home—he'll soon realize that *"Puppy, Come!"* means *"End of fun, time for home!"*

- Never let your Beagle off the line unless you are 100 percent sure that, whatever the distraction, you can call him back and he will come. Never let him off in an area where there are roads nearby. If you are confident in his recall, practice letting him off the leash in safe, enclosed areas first, such as on a tennis court, in a training club's grounds, or in a friend's yard (making sure it is escape-proof).

- Many people just won't risk letting their dogs run free. It's a personal decision, based on your dog's obedience, but also your own risk assessment. Perhaps talk to your breeder if you need help in reaching a decision.

THE STAY EXERCISE

The Stay exercise should be built up gradually.

With practice, your Beagle should stay in the **Stand**, the **Sit** and the **Down**.

STAY

This is another exercise that needs a fair amount of practice, as it just isn't in a Beagle puppy's nature to want to sit and stay in one spot for more than a couple of seconds! As with all training, however, if you show your puppy that it is worth his while to apply himself, and that he can have lots of fun after he's done as you wish, you should be successful.

- Ask your Beagle to sit or lie down (see above).
- Quickly walk one step away, say *"Stay,"* and give the corresponding hand signal (your arm outstretched toward him, with your palm held up. This body language literally reinforces that you want to keep him away.
- Click and treat him, then quickly step back to him, and give him lots of praise.
- Practice this little and often, keeping the *Stays* very short—in distance and in time.

- After practicing for just five or ten minutes, have a running around game together, so he can let off steam.
- When he has mastered staying on the spot at one step away for a short time, then increase the time he has to stay from a couple of seconds to a count of ten.
- When he's mastered this, try two steps away for five seconds, then, two steps away at ten seconds, three steps at five seconds, and so on.
- Do not rush. Take each stage slowly, so that you gradually build up to being able to get your Beagle to stay at some distance from you, for a fair length of time.
- If your Beagle starts breaking the *Stay*, then go back down a stage. For example, if he just won't stay at 15 steps from you for 20 seconds, try 12 steps for ten seconds again, and build up from there.

LEAD TRAINING

Initial reluctance to lead training can be overcome by offering treats, or playing with a toy.

WALKS

Beagles love their walks. Although it may be a few weeks before you can take your puppy out in public (once he has had his vaccinations and you have had the go-ahead from your veterinarian), you can get a head start by teaching him to accept the leash in your backyard.

- First, get the puppy used to wearing a collar. Initially, he may find it cumbersome, and may scratch at it, and try to rub it off by wriggling around on the floor, but distract him with a game, or some easy training exercises (such as *Sit*). If you put it on him for short, but frequent, sessions, and gradually increase the time that it is left on, he will soon get used to it, and will probably forget that it's on.

- When he is used to wearing his collar, then it's time to introduce the lead. Attach the lead, and then let the puppy have a sniff and a walk around the yard. Follow him wherever he goes, making sure you keep the lead loose, so that he doesn't even realize he's attached to it.

- After a few short sessions like this, take the lead—literally! Walk slowly, in a straight line, and encourage the puppy to come with you. Be encouraging, tapping your thigh, and calling his name, and click, treat, and praise him when he walks next to you with the lead loose.

- If the puppy pulls ahead, don't pull him back. Just stop, encourage him to come and sit next to you, and then set off again.

- When he is walking calmly by your side, say *"Heel"* so that he learns what this word means (walking close to your left leg, neither pulling forward nor lagging behind).

- When you can take your puppy out in public (once your veterinarian has given the go-ahead after the series of vaccinations), be warned that he is likely to want to pull ahead, to explore the new places he is visiting. Be calm, take things slowly, and don't let him bully you into walking faster than you want to go. If he pulls, stop. Call him back, then start again.

EXCESSIVE BARKING

Beagles can like the sound of their own voices. It's important, when you first get your puppy, that you teach him to be quiet on command. It may be easier said than done, but with consistent, early training, you may get there in the end.

Every time your Beagle barks inappropriately, say *"No"* calmly but firmly. Do not shout or get overexcited, as this will actually invite him to be noisy. For example, if your dog is barking because someone walked past the house, he may think that your yelling is "human barking" and that you are worried about the person too. Your dog will then join in with you, to make sure the potential intruder is warned off!

EASY DOES IT!

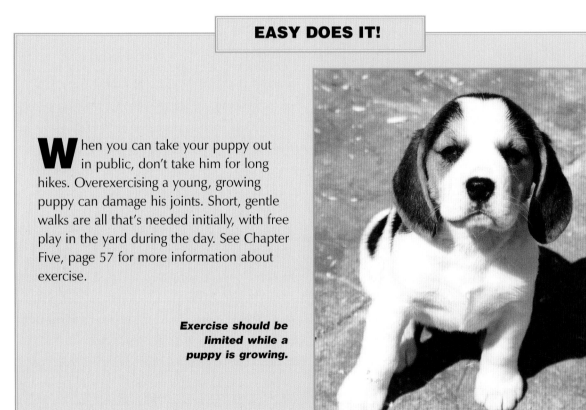

When you can take your puppy out in public, don't take him for long hikes. Overexercising a young, growing puppy can damage his joints. Short, gentle walks are all that's needed initially, with free play in the yard during the day. See Chapter Five, page 57 for more information about exercise.

Exercise should be limited while a puppy is growing.

The Beagle can be more vocal than you would like, so it is best to nip this habit in the bud.

After saying *"No,"* calmly distract your dog. Call him to you, and get him to do some training exercises, such as *Sit*. Give praise and a reward when he complies with your requests.

As with any training, the most important factor is to be consistent. Even if you are tired or busy, always follow the same routine if your Beagle barks. With time, he should give up being noisy; some dogs even give one bark and then find their owner and sit in front of him, anticipating a training session!

Remember, barking is a dog's way of communicating. He may bark through loneliness, fear, pain, or even boredom. If your dog is making excessive noise, try to get to the bottom of why he is doing so. A trip to the veterinarian, to eliminate any health reasons, may be worthwhile. If given the all-clear, and if your training is not working, your veterinarian can refer your dog to a trainer or behaviorist, to help you get some peace at last!

SOCIALIZATION

Exposing your young Beagle to as many different situations as possible is extremely important. As soon as it is safe to take him out and about, show him as much of life as you can, so that it will hold no fear for him when he is older.

Take him to bus and train stations, introduce him to well-behaved dogs and children, walk him through a bustling market. Be as comprehensive as you can.

Even before he is protected by his vaccinations, you can drive him around in the car, or carry him in your arms, so that he can see the outside world.

Always act confidently, as your Beagle will often look to you for guidance on how he should react to new experiences. If you are nervous about how he will respond, he will detect your anxiety.

CHAPTER FIVE

CARING FOR YOUR BEAGLE

Beagles are not high-maintenance dogs. Their coats are easy to care for and they are not usually fussy about what they eat—far from it. Most of your time will be spent training your dog, and just enjoying life together. However, every dog requires regular checks and basic care, and it's important to get into a good routine from the start.

FEEDING

If you pick up your Beagle puppy when he is eight weeks old, you will probably be giving him four meals a day. This is usually reduced to three meals (breakfast, lunch, and dinner) by 12 weeks, and reduced further down to two meals (breakfast and supper) by six months of age. Some owners like to cut this down to one meal a day by eight months, but most prefer to continue with two throughout the dog's life. Of course, as the number of meals is reduced, the other meals are made larger to compensate.

Every dog is an individual. For example, some will start to show less interest in their lunch earlier than others. Be guided by your dog— flexibility is the key.

Your breeder should have provided you with a detailed diet sheet, giving information on exactly what to feed and when, together with advice about reducing the number of meals.

Any changes to the diet should be made gradually.

Beagles love their food, so it is not hard to find a suitable diet.

Follow the breeder's advice, and if you have any questions, contact him or her; they should be more than happy to help.

Diet change

If your Beagle is not thriving on the food that has been recommended by the breeder, ask the breeder's advice. It could be that a change of food is necessary. If you are having trouble finding the food, the breeder may be able to advise you on a suitable alternative.

Changing a dog or puppy's food should always be done gradually. With puppies, especially, their body gets used to what it is fed, and a sudden change can result in stomach upsets. Always wait until the puppy is comfortably settled in his new home before considering a change. Stress also causes digestive problems, and if the puppy has to cope with a new home and family, together with a different food, you are asking for trouble.

If you do need to change his diet, after a couple of months of him being with you (and with the blessing of your breeder), then make sure the diet is nutritious, with everything your puppy needs to grow into a healthy adult. Some people feed meat and kibble biscuits; others swear by homemade diets of fresh meat and vegetables. If choosing the latter, discuss the diet with your veterinarian, to ensure that you will be providing all the vitamins and minerals your Beagle will need.

Complete diets are very popular and are readily available. They provide all the nutrients a dog needs, and, being in the form of dry food, are very convenient to use. You just measure out the recommended amount and away you go! Most brands have different life stages, with

DRINKING WATER

Water makes up 70 percent of a dog's body weight, so it is crucial for his health. Always make sure that your Beagle has access to a bowl of fresh water. If you are traveling in the car, take a bottle of water and a bowl with you. It's important that he can quench his thirst, especially in warm weather.

If feeding a complete, dry diet, your dog will drink more water than if he is fed canned dog food, which has a higher moisture content.

If you notice that your dog is drinking more or less, consult your veterinarian, as a change in eating and drinking habits should always be investigated in case it is indicative of an underlying health problem.

puppy, adult, light (low-calorie), and senior varieties, to accommodate a dog's changing nutritional needs throughout his life.

- When changing a diet, do so very gradually to give your Beagle's body time to adjust.
- Add a spoonful of the new food to your Beagle's normal meal, giving him a spoonful less of the previous food.
- Over the course of a week to 10 days, gradually increase the amount of new food, and decrease the amount of the previous food, until, eventually, a complete changeover has been accomplished.
- If your dog shows any adverse effects during the changeover, or once he is on his new diet, consult your veterinarian, as your dog may have a food allergy.

Fighting the flab

Beagles love their grub! Some breeds eat to live, but the Beagle definitely falls into the "live to eat" camp! This is a great advantage in some respects, dealing with a fussy eater can be very time-consuming and stressful, but the downside is that you will have to monitor carefully what your Beagle eats.

If left to his own devices, a Beagle will eat and eat and eat, so weigh out exactly what he should have for each meal, and don't be persuaded to give him more. Never give in to begging. If your Beagle sits at your feet when you are eating, and paws at you for food, remove him to another room. If you (or your family) accidentally drop some food on the floor, your dog will gobble it up before you know it, which

It is hard to resist those melting brown eyes, but you must consider the health risks if your Beagle becomes obese.

HEALTHY TREATS

When training your Beagle, food is a great reward to use. However, make sure you take the treats into consideration as part of his overall daily intake of food, and reduce the amount given for his meals accordingly.

Fresh fruit and vegetables also make good training treats. Cubes of raw carrot or apple, for example, are often enjoyed as much as kibble-based treats. However, do not feed grapes, as some dogs have had serious reactions to them. Similarly, chocolate intended for human consumption should never be given, as it contains theobromine, which can be deadly to dogs.

The Beagle should look lean and athletic.

will inadvertantly reward him for his dining-room vigil.

You should also be aware of what food your Beagle can steal. If you leave some cookies on the coffee table, or meat to cool on the kitchen counter, don't expect them to be there when you return!

Don't fall into the trap of showing your Beagle love through food—you could end up killing him with your "kindness." Being overweight not only adversely affects a dog's quality of life (with joint and mobility problems) but also the length of it. Obesity puts undue pressure on the heart and contributes to many health conditions.

A fit, healthy, adult Beagle will have a clear waist when viewed from above, and you should be able to feel his ribs when you run your fingers along his side. If your Beagle loses his waist, and his ribs cannot be felt easily, it's time to shed those pounds.

Most veterinarians offer diet clinics, run by veterinary technicians, with regular weigh-in sessions, plus special advice on losing excess weight. You may also be recommended to change your dog's diet to a "light" variety.

Weighing your dog every week, when you perform your other general health checks, is a good routine to get into, as, too often, the weight can creep on unnoticed.

EXERCISE

One of the great joys of dog ownership is taking your pet out for a relaxing walk, to enjoy the great outdoors, to bond with your dog, and to unwind from a stressful day. Your Beagle will certainly enjoy this quality time with you, although he will be quickly distracted by other dogs or people on his walk, and will probably want to run off and play with his new friends, or chase squirrels instead!

As discussed in Chapter Four, the Beagle's recall is notoriously bad, so never let your dog off the lead unless you are certain that he will come back immediately when you call. If he cannot be trusted off-lead, invest in an extending lead, which will give him some degree of freedom, while you can still retain ultimate control.

Whether on lead or off, it's important that your Beagle's exercise is varied, so that his mind and body are stimulated. It'll keep you from becoming bored with the same old walk too!

- Vary where you walk, and the routes you take.
- If your Beagle enjoys a dip, find out if there are any canine hydrotherapy pools in your area (your veterinarian may be able to recommend one), so your dog can swim in a controlled, safe environment.
- Take a toy with you on a walk, to throw for your dog, and teach him to retrieve.
- With yard-based exercise, be aware that many Beagles like to do their own little horticulture, which involves a lot of digging! Fence off any prized plants, and consider giving your dog a special area in the yard where he can dig to his heart's content. A children's sandbox, filled with earth, is often popular, especially if you bury some of your dog's toys in it for him to excavate.

When your Beagle gets a scent, he may become deaf to your calls.

EXERCISE

The Beagle loves to run and play, and an outing is considered the high spot of the day!

Care should be taken not to overexert a growing puppy. He should not be taken out to public places until he is fully protected by his vaccinations. When your veterinarian gives you the all-clear, then, until six months of age, your Beagle needs only to play in the yard, together with two short walks on the leash (as much for socialization and training as for his own exercise needs).

Thereafter, gently increase his exercise sessions. Don't jump from a five-minute walk around the block one day, to a five-mile hike the next. Your Beagle puppy needs to build up his strength and stamina gradually so as not to put undue pressure on his developing joints.

After they are fully grown (around 12–18 months), Beagles will usually take as much exercise as they can get!

To begin with, your puppy will get all the exercise he needs playing in the yard.

Work at your recall training, then you can allow your Beagle the chance to explore new places.

GROOMING

The Beagle has a short, dense, waterproof coat, which is very easy to maintain, requiring only a quick brushing with a bristle brush or a hound glove to remove dead hairs and to keep the dog looking well groomed. Some breeders recommend running a chamois leather over the coat at the end of the grooming session to give the coat a professional shine.

Bathing

If the dog gets muddy, usually it is sufficient to let him dry and then to brush off the mud. However, you might need to use a damp cloth to remove any bits of dirt that have stubbornly clung to the coat.

- Beagles very rarely need a bath, but if your dog rolls in something particularly smelly, or you think he could do with freshening up, put him in the bath (or, if it's easier, a shower stall), and wet the coat thoroughly with warm water.
- Use a rubber mat in the bath/shower, so the dog doesn't slip.
- A shower hose is good for giving a continuous stream of clean water, and is more convenient than using endless containers of bathwater.
- When the coat is wet through, use a mild shampoo intended for dogs, and then rinse thoroughly, until there are no soapy suds left in the coat.
- Be careful not to get any soap in the dog's eyes, as it will need rinsing out, which most dogs hate. Lather as high as the neck and

> ### TIP!
>
> **S**ome adult dogs hate to be bathed, and it can be a two-person job, with the dog endlessly struggling to escape the tub. Giving your puppy a bath or two when he's young, and making sure he is given treats and lots of praise, will help him to perceive bathtime as fun time!

avoid the head area.

- Then rub the coat through with a hound glove to remove any loose hairs, and rinse through again.
- Use a thick, absorbent towel to remove most of the moisture before you bring him out of the bath/shower.
- It's usually sufficient to let the rest of the coat dry naturally, keeping the dog in a warm room so he doesn't become chilled.
- If you need to speed up the drying process, you can use a hairdryer. However, make sure that it is held a fair distance away from the dog, so you do not burn his skin with the hot air.
- Do not point the dryer at one point on the dog for any length of time. Keep it moving all over the dog.

Dental care

It's important to brush your dog's teeth at least a couple of times a week. This comes as a surprise to some people, who claim that wild dogs don't brush their teeth, so domestic dogs don't need to either. However, pet dogs have a very different lifestyle than when their ancestors hunted for their own food. They would tear up raw meat, and crunch on bones, which would naturally remove any plaque and prevent the buildup of tartar. Our modern dog is given his food in his bowl, and although dry food helps to remove some plaque, it isn't sufficient by itself.

Veterinarians and pet shops sell toothbrushes and pastes specifically for use in dogs. Do not use "human" toothpaste, which contains fluoride. It is not intended to be swallowed, and dogs are not very good at spitting out! Instead, use special canine toothpaste, which comes in a range of mouthwatering varieties—some are even beef or chicken-flavored!

If you get your young Beagle puppy used to having his teeth brushed from a young age, he will quickly learn to accept it. Give plenty of praise, and keep the dental sessions short, always finishing up with a (tooth-friendly, natural) treat, and even adult dogs will learn to sit still while it is being done.

As well as specially formulated dental chews, there are gels/pastes on the market that contain enzymes that help to keep plaque off dogs' teeth. Ask your veterinarian for details.

Nail art

Once a week, check your Beagle's nails to make sure they don't need trimming. If your Beagle is exercised regularly on a hard surface, the nails should wear down naturally. If your Beagle is walked mostly on soft ground, the nails may need to be cut.

Most Beagles' nails are white, which makes it easy to see the quick (the blood supply). If you accidentally cut the quick, it will bleed profusely and will be sore for your dog, so snip only a little off the nail at a time. If they are still too long, you can always go back and snip off a fraction more. Guillotine-type nail clippers are easy to use, as you can see exactly how much you are cutting.

Some people prefer to file the nails, either manually with an emery board (which is very time-consuming), or with an electric nail filer. However, a small number of dogs object to the vibrating sensation.

- If your Beagle's nails do need cutting, choose a time when he is relaxed, such as after a meal.
- If he is a wriggler, enlist the help of a family member or friend, to restrain the dog while you do the snipping.
- Your Beagle's dewclaws (the claws high up the foot) should have been removed. If they have not been, do keep a careful check on them to ensure that they don't grow too long and curl around into the foot.
- Always finish with a treat and lots of praise. Your Beagle will remember the rewards next time and is more likely to cooperate.
- If you are at all uncertain about the procedure, ask your veterinarian to show you how to do it.

Other checks

After checking your Beagle's nails, give him a quick once-over:

The Beagle is a low-maintenance breed in terms of coat care.

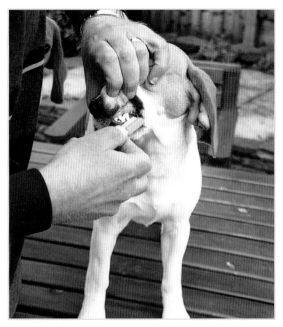

Teeth need to be brushed on a regular basis.

The tips of the nails can be trimmed using guillotine-type nail clippers.

Check the ears, and clean them if necessary.

- Inspect his mouth and teeth. If he has bad breath, he may need a dental examination from your veterinarian. Also check for any signs or inflammation and soreness.
- Check his feet and pads for any cuts or in case anything has lodged between his toes. Grass awns can easily get embedded into the tissue, and need removing before they work themselves in further.
- Check under his tail, to make sure his bottom is clean. Any signs of soreness should be reported to your veterinarian.
- When you groom your dog, look through his coat for any evidence of parasites. Ticks should be removed with special tick tweezers, which remove the whole tick. If you just pull at the tick with ordinary tweezers, you can leave the head embedded under the skin. Fleas or other parasites should be treated appropriately (see Chapter Nine).
- Any lumps or bumps should be checked by your veterinarian.
- Check your dog's ears, and clean them with an ear cleaner if necessary. If the ears are dirty, red, sore, or if your dog keeps scratching at them, he may have an infection, and should be seen by a veterinarian.

ADOLESCENT CARE

From between 6 and 24 months, the Beagle experiences adolescence, the transition phase from puppyhood to adulthood. During this time, dogs grow physically (though not always mentally!), and also become sexually mature. Because of the surge of sex hormones racing around their bodies, your sweet little Beagle puppy may develop horns for a few months and become a little monster. This is normal!

During adolescence, dogs can test the boundaries, seeing how far they can go with their owner. Again, this is perfectly normal, and is very similar to human adolescence. Just be patient and consistent. If your Beagle isn't allowed on your furniture, for example, don't turn a blind eye just to have a quiet life. Ask him to get off, even if it means doing it 20 times a day. If you relent on one issue, you may have to give way on other house rules too, and your dog will just become more and more confused, and will lose confidence in your leadership.

Many owners notice no differences in their dogs during the teenage phase, so you might be lucky, but it is good to be prepared. Warn other family members too, so you all put on a united front. If you insist that your Beagle cannot sleep on the sofa, but your partner ignores a transgression of the rules, then you will be fighting a losing battle. If your Beagle learns that he will always be asked to get off the sofa, no matter what, then he'll soon figure out that there's no point getting on it.

The same principle applies to all other house rules, such as begging, jumping up on people, etc. Ignore the dog, and do not give him attention when he is performing these actions. Even shouting at him, or pushing him down constitutes attention, so just turn away, without looking at him. Instead, give him lots of attention when he sits quietly, or greets people without jumping up.

Do not underestimate the power of ignoring undesirable behavior, such as jumping up. As far as the dog is concerned, attention is rewarding, even if you are telling him off. As soon as the dog is responding correctly—in this case, standing with all four feet on the ground—you can reward him by giving him praise and attention.

Neutering

Neutering means surgically preventing a female or a male from being able to have or sire puppies. It can prevent some undesirable behavior, such as mounting, but it is not a universal "cure-all." If your dog is aggressive with other dogs, neutering may help to calm him down, but it may not; socialization and training are probably going to be more effective. If your dog already has a behavior problem, such as mounting or aggression, neutering may not help at all if that behavior has become ingrained.

It is best to discuss neutering with your veterinarian. He or she may be able to get to the source of the problem (or may refer you to a behaviorist).

Neutering should still be considered, regardless of your dog's behavior. There are pros and cons, so weigh all the factors and discuss them with your veterinarian, in order to reach an informed decision.

• Neutering prevents unwanted puppies from being born. There are thousands and thousands of dogs in rescue shelters that were unwanted

There are many health benefits associated with neutering.

and that are desperate for homes. One accidental mating can add to their numbers.

- Intact (unneutered) males and females are prone to straying to find a mate. Given the breed's poor traffic sense and recall, you may never recover your Beagle.

- Owning a neutered animal is more convenient for the owner. A female will need to be kept away from all other dogs when she is in heat (usually twice a year). This can be problematic if you own an intact male dog.

- Most females keep themselves very clean, but there will inevitably be some bloody discharge, which can be a problem if you have pale carpets or other furnishings.

- Neutering has many health benefits, such as reducing the incidence of mammary tumors and removing the risk of life-threatening pyometra (infection of the uterus) in females, and in removing the chance of prostate cancer in males.

- Neutering can have negative effects. Anesthetics can present a risk. Modern anesthetics are incredibly effective, and the risks are neglible, but they must be considered.

- Neutering sometimes results in the male or female being slightly less active. This can lead to weight gain, unless the dog's diet is adjusted.

- Urinary incontinence following spaying of the female does occur in the breed, but is not that common. It is often associated with obesity. In middle-aged spayed females, urinary incontinence is usually due to a combination of factors, including lack of muscle tone in the urethral sphincter, short urethra, and malpositioned bladder. Surgery can sometimes result in a permanent cure for the problem or, more commonly, medical treatment involving tablets prescribed by your veterinarian.

• Recently, some people have claimed that there is an ethical argument against altering a dog just for the sake of the owner's convenience. However, those who disagree point to the health benefits that the dog can enjoy.

THE OLDER DOG

The average lifespan for the Beagle is between 12 and 14 years. Cancer can be a problem in the breed, but if a dog doesn't fall victim to it, he may go on to his high teens.

A Beagle usually reaches double figures before he even begins to show signs of slowing up a little. There may be a little graying around the muzzle, he may become a little arthritic, and his hearing and sight may deteriorate a little, but most dogs continue to have the great Beagle zest of life as they always have done.

The older Beagle deserves special consideration.

- With older dogs, make sure their bed is in a warm, draft-free location. The cold can play havoc with arthritis.
- When a dog ages, everything begins to slow down a little, including the digestive system. Consider splitting your dog's daily food allocation into three meals, and speak to your veterinarian about whether the diet you are feeding is the best for your dog's age and condition. It might be worth considering switching to a "senior" variety.
- Keep a close eye on your dog's weight. If his metabolism starts slowing down, especially if he is exercising less, his food allocation may need to be reduced too.
- Shorter exercise periods may also be worth thinking about, but only if your Beagle needs it. Most continue with their usual long walks well into old age.
- Weekly health checks are very important with older dogs, so you can pick up any early signs of ill health. Veterinary checks every six months are also advised.
- If your Beagle feels the need to sleep more, let him, and make sure he is not disturbed by youngsters (canine or human).

SAYING GOOD-BYE

Loving—and being loved by—a Beagle is one of life's greatest experiences; losing him is one of the saddest. It is an unfortunate fact that dogs do not live as long as humans do, so having to say good-bye to your faithful companion is inevitable. Hopefully, it will not be for many, many years, but when the time comes, and your dog can no longer be helped by your veterinarian, it is important not to let your Beagle suffer. It is your ultimate responsibility, as a loving pet owner, to ensure that your dog dies peacefully and with dignity. This is achieved through euthanasia, a deep sleep followed almost immediately by death.

The veterinarian staff will help to support you through the procedure, and afterward. He or she can also discuss with you what you would like to do with the body. Some people like to have their animals cremated, and either keep the ashes, or scatter them on their dog's favorite walk. Others like to bury their dog in a pet cemetery, and some people prefer to leave the body with the veterinarian.

Dealing with the great sense of loss after losing a dog is very difficult. No matter how many times you lose a pet, it is something you never get used to. Talking to family and friends can help with the grieving process, and your veterinarian will be able to give you details of pet-loss counseling services.

Ann Phillips from Worcestershire, England, spent a wonderful 16 years with Hudson, described as her "special boy," before she finally had to say good-bye.

"I had Hudson from when he was six weeks old," she recalls. "He was sired by a dog of mine, and I had the pick of the litter from the moment the puppies were born. I had bred his father, grandfather and great-grandmother, and they were all long-lived, which, in a breed prone to cancer, is a blessing.

"Hudson was a one-person dog. He came everywhere with me from the time he was tiny, and traveled well. He wasn't your typical Beagle—he was obedient and biddable to begin with. I put this down to the fact that, when he was young, I did a lot of work with Golden Retrievers. I had half a dozen of them for four years, and Hudson seemed to grow up thinking he was a Golden. All his life, he would greet a Golden with great enthusiasm, and would think other Beagles were very strange indeed!

"It was only in the last three years of his life that he began to show signs of getting older. He developed arthritis in his back legs, but we managed to control it. Some people didn't even realize Hudson had a problem.

SLOWING DOWN

"In the last year, when he was 15, he did start to slow down. The stairs became difficult for him to manage, and I would have to lift him into and out of the car. But he enjoyed a walk every day, even until the day he died.

"As Hudson got older, he became more demanding. He had always been a dog that made his presence felt, and, by the age of six

Hudson enjoying his 16th birthday party.

months had learned to bark if a door was closed to him. By the time he reached his teens, he didn't just bark and wait politely; the older he became, the more he barked. If the weather was cold, the bark had an irritated tone to it, becoming louder and more urgent the longer he waited. It was the utter quiet that was the hardest to bear after his death.

"Another aspect of old age was a change of attitude to food. Hudson was never a greedy Beagle. He enjoyed his food but didn't bolt it down, but, from about 12 years of age, food became more important to him, and the demanding bark became a feature of feeding times. With the onset of very old age, I split his main meal into two, giving half at lunchtime, so as not to overload his digestive system. This appealed to him greatly, giving him much more opportunity to make noise!

FOOD, GLORIOUS FOOD
"The other change of heart with regard to food was his sudden desire to accept it from wherever it was offered. This was in direct contrast to his youth, when he would not take anything from people he didn't know well. This, in turn, led to occasional stealing, if the occasion presented itself, and a great deal of mock embarrassment on his behalf if discovered.

"For his 16th birthday, I had a little party for him, with friends and family. Hudson always loved opening presents. Every Christmas, he would dive under the tree and unwrap anything he could, he was worse than a small child. For his birthday, his presents mostly consisted of things to eat, and a squeaky toy. He loved squeakies, especially his snowman toy. He could also distinguish between his toys. Some people say dogs are color-blind, but it's not true. Hudson had two balls, which were identical apart from their color. If I asked him to fetch his red ball, he would get it—even if both balls were together; the same with the blue one—he would be right every time!

"The Sunday before Hudson died, he won Best Veteran at a show. On Wednesday, I had been in town, and so he stayed with some friends who looked after him if I needed to go away. I picked him up at 5 P.M., and he had a seizure within an hour of my picking him up. I suspect he had a brain tumor. The seizure seemed to switch everything off. When he had a second seizure, I decided enough was enough—it was time to let him go.

FOREVER FRIENDS
"It was a mercy, really. The following week, I was due to be in Australia. Had he died at my friends' house, they would have felt terrible, and so would I. This way, I was with him from the beginning through to the end.

"Hudson is still with me. I have his ashes in my home, which I find very comforting. My other dogs were buried in my yard, but then I moved. This way, he will always be with me, wherever I am.

"Hudson was a very special dog. Some people don't get a relationship like that in a lifetime. It hurt to lose him, but it was an honor to have shared my life with him."

CHAPTER SIX

BROADENING HORIZONS

The Beagle was bred to work, so it should come as no surprise that this active breed is happiest when kept busy. Whatever your age, income, fitness, or time availability, there is bound to be something to suit you and your dog.

CANINE GOOD CITIZEN

The Canine Good Citizen Award is run by the Kennel Club in the UK and the American Kennel Club in the United States. The program aims to encourage responsible dog ownership and to educate owners about the benefits of having a well-behaved pet.

The American Kennel Club runs a two-part program, at the end of which the dog must pass an examination made up of 10 tests that cover basic behavior and control.

In the UK, there are grades—puppy foundation, bronze, silver, and gold—with the pass criteria becoming steadily harder as the dog progresses through them:

- Puppy foundation
- Bronze award
- Silver award
- Gold award.

If you enroll in the program, you will have to demonstrate that your dog can behave in a calm, controlled, and confident manner in a variety of situations, including:

- Being approached and petted by a stranger
- Getting in and out of a car safely
- Meeting another dog
- Being groomed and handled
- Responding to a number of basic commands (such as *"Sit," "Down,"* etc.)
- Walking on a loose leash in a controlled manner.

Many training clubs now offer Good Citizen programs as a part of their training, and, in most cases, it is relatively easy to join a club fairly close to your home. If you are interested

The Good Citizen tests are an excellent way of training your Beagle in good manners and obedience.

in finding out more, your national kennel club will be able to provide you with details of clubs in your area.

COMPETITIVE OBEDIENCE

Beagles are intelligent, athletic dogs, and they respond well to Obedience training. They may not be one of the best-known or "typical" Obedience breeds, but those Beagles that take part, perform very well. However, even if you never win a competition, you will at least have the benefit of owning an extremely well-trained Beagle!

Beagles are renowned for being stubborn.

However, this is simply due to a breakdown in communication between dog and owner. When a Beagle is stubborn, he is simply telling his owner that, as far as he is concerned, he isn't being given enough motivation to do what his owner wants. Find the right motivating factor, and your Beagle will suddenly seem intent on pleasing you.

Being a scenthound, interesting smells, such as food, tend to work best as motivators. Many trainers advocate a graded system of treats, where "everyday" treats are used for basic commands that your Beagle will respond to quite easily, and "extraspecial" treats, such as a particularly tasty piece of liver, are used for commands that you normally can't get your Beagle to do at all. The average Beagle is highly intelligent, and it won't be long before he catches on to the fact that doing something he may not necessarily be that anxious to do is worth it because of the extraspecial treat he will get at the end.

Getting started

If you are interested in taking part in Obedience, join a training class—your national kennel club will be able to provide you with details. Do not be afraid to visit several classes before committing yourself to one. Ask as many questions as you can, and, if possible, try to witness a class in action. Make sure you choose a class where positive training methods are used. It also helps if you choose a trainer who has some experience with Beagles, although this is not a fundamental prerequisite.

Susan Arden, from North Lanarkshire, Scotland, has kept Beagles since her teens and has remained a devoted fan of the breed ever since.

"When my mom finally allowed my sister, Hazel, and me to have a dog, she laid down some conditions: the dog had to be smallish, smooth-coated, friendly, and pleasing to look at. We wanted a small dog that 'thinks big,' and Beagles seemed to be the ideal choice. Hazel and I had really enjoyed training our cats to come when called, to sit, to stay, to walk at heel, to give a paw on request, and to jump through homemade agility courses we set, and we greatly looked forward to teaching our two new Beagles—Gemma (Newlin Picnic) and Katie (Dunnybrae Oyster)—to do the same.

"I was introduced to Obedience through a friend named Liz. She was a regular in the show ring and at Obedience competitions, and she took us along to our local dog training club, which ran ring training and Obedience classes. We also found out about Working Trials, and it wasn't long before our Beagles were trying all three disciplines!

"At the age of 10 months, Katie and Gemma gave a successful Obedience demonstration at the Scottish Beagle Club Championship Show. A few months later, we entered our first Beginners Obedience competition, and, out of more than 40 entrants, we took first and second place. We were absolutely delighted! Now, I am working with Katie's great-grandson, Miles (Champion Madika Nut Case), who is turning out to be my star.

"Beagles are not difficult to train for Obedience, provided that you lay down the ground rules at an early age. Make them *Sit* and *Wait* before giving them a treat, give them lots of praise and a treat when you call them and they come to you. Beagles generally love their food, and if you keep a treat in your hand while practicing heelwork, you'll be surprised at how quickly they grasp the idea. Initially, you should give them a treat every time they do the right thing, but then you need to start withdrawing the rewards slowly, so that they are never sure when they will or won't get one. This is important because, sadly, treats are not allowed in competition.

"It is also important not to overtrain. Beagles are intelligent dogs but they can lose interest, so train only in short, 10-minute bursts. I find that formal training twice a week works best for my Beagles. You can incorporate a lot of other training into your daily life, such as making the dog *Wait* before jumping in and out of the car, not to pull at the leash, to *Sit* before being given a meal, and so on. This also helps you to achieve the end result of a well-behaved house pet, too.

Continued overleaf

How it all started: Gemma and Katie winning at their first Obedience competition.

" The best aspect of competing with a Beagle is the looks people give you. "

Susan doing a Recall with Miles.

"If you can master the basics, Competitive Obedience is really just an extension of this, with a lot more accuracy. For example, *Sits* need to be straight, and there must be no wide turns on the heelwork. However, even at this level it should be fun and rewarding. Instead of giving the dog the treat for coming when called, make him Present to you properly—that is, sit dead straight in front of you—and then give him the treat. All my Beagles know the meaning of 'In straight.'

"Miles showed early promise from the start. He had nice, close heelwork, accurate *Sits,* and he was always happy. He sailed through his Beginners class after attending for only three weeks. He later went on to win the Beginners section of our club competition, and we were also named dog and handler of the year. Since then, he has won eight firsts out of 12 competitions. At one show, I entered both the Intermediate and Advance sections, and we won both. What a day! I was incredibly proud of him.

"Miles can have his moments, however. At one competition he was performing brilliantly,

and then came the *Stays.* Just as I was settling him out of sight for the *Sit-Stay,* the Whippets in another area started their race. Miles took off to join them, leaving me standing in the ring with no dog! I managed to retrieve him and try again, only for Miles to fly past me back on his way to the Whippets.

"If you decide to compete with a Beagle, you need to remember that he is a scenthound, and his nose can sometimes get the better of him. A simple rustle of a paper bag from a ringside spectator and your Beagle can end up acting as if he hasn't been fed for a week!

"The best aspect of competing with a Beagle is the looks people give you; it's as if you're in the wrong place. Then, you come out of the ring, with your dog having performed brilliantly, and no one seems able to believe that the Beagle 'did it.' At my first competition with Miles, which we won, the judge announced that, if anyone had told her a Beagle would be the winner, she wouldn't have believed them!"

A group Stay with Miles (left), Molly, Milly, Daisy, and Poppy.

Glenn Laffy's two Beagles, Chips (eight-year-old Marianne Daisy Chips CD), and Rudy (eight-month-old Echo Run Flying Ace), descend from stars of Field Trials and the show ring. Here Glenn describes how his Beagles trained him.

"I would say that Beagles chose me for Obedience," says Glenn, from Farwell, Michigan. "Chips was my first Beagle, and she didn't take long to train me. Although I knew a little bit about basic dog training when I got Chips, I knew nothing about Competitive Obedience. I didn't even know it existed. Chips was about seven months old when I got her, and we started training. Then, when she was about three years old, we went to a dog show. As we wandered from ring to ring, I came across dogs doing heeling patterns,

Glenn with his Obedience-trained Beagles Chips and Rudy.

retrieving dumbbells, performing long *Sits* and *Downs,* and doing all sorts of things very different from what I'd seen in the conformation rings. I was fascinated! Wondering what it was all about, I stopped a few exhibitors and asked some questions, and that's how I found out about Obedience.

"After the show, I found myself thinking 'My dogs could do that, if we worked at it enough,' so I got hold of a copy of the AKC Obedience rules and began reading them. As far as I could see, Competitive Obedience was really an extension of basic training—*Sits, Downs,* and *Stays* are all exercises you cover with any puppy. The degree of precision may be higher, and the exercises more demanding, but the basic principles are just the same. I decided to give it a try.

"Initially, I taught myself with books and video tapes. It didn't occur to me to find a club, which I think now was a mistake. Some of the early methods I used didn't work very well, and they also set in place some bad habits that later proved very hard to break. Eventually, I heard about a nearby training club and decided to enroll.

"Once I joined the class, things really started to happen. I found the classes extremely helpful, and I'd highly recommend proper training classes to anyone interested in Obedience. The class I attended used positive training methods, which, for Beagles, work far better than some of the more traditional methods, which can involve a certain amount of coercion. When I started teaching Chips heelwork, I used the old-fashioned 'tug and jerk' method, so that she would realize that pulling me would result only in a sharp tug of the leash—not very pleasant. Chips began to hate heelwork. Even now, it is something of our nemesis, but since we have been using positive training methods to teach heelwork, she has really improved.

Continued overleaf

> **Attention training can, and should, be taught very early on.**

ATTENTION TO DETAIL

"One of the biggest advantages from joining the class was being taught proper attention training. Attention training can, and should, be taught very early on. It involves having the Beagle look directly into the trainer's eyes, with the command *'Watch me!'* or something similar. Beagles have a tendency to get sidetracked by the desire to sniff, and their independent minds need to be given focus. Attention training is a way of overcoming this, and, of course, if your Beagle is looking at you for his next command, he is far less likely to notice anything that might prove to be too much temptation. I'm really glad that I got proper help training Chips. One of my proudest moments with her came when she achieved her Companion Dog title from the AKC. It was the biggest thrill.

"Chips has done well at Obedience, but her nose can sometimes get her into trouble. At one Open trial, we were in the middle of a Retrieve exercise when I noticed a lady on the sidelines

A perfect Retrieve—but Beagles can be full of surprises.

eating a sandwich. Unfortunately, Chips noticed too! When I commanded her to *'Fetch,'* she ran right up to the lady and stood on her hindlegs, begging for a bite.

DOGGIE DIVERSIONS

"At another Open, again during a Retrieve exercise, I commanded Chips to fetch the dumbbell from over the high jump. She jumped beautifully, but then decided to pay a visit to the judge rather than retrieve the dumbbell. After sitting patiently by the judge for a while, she seemed to realize that she wasn't going to get anything, so she returned to the dumbbell, picked it up, came back over the jump, and sat looking up at me as if nothing had happened! We lost some points for that, but I was just relieved that Chips finished the job.

"Beagles are not a natural retrieving breed, and if you have one that really dislikes it, it can be a problem. Chips didn't like it, and we had to do a lot of training to overcome it. I had to use a process called 'back-chaining,' which involved breaking the exercise down into various elements and teaching them separately. In Chips' case, we had to go right back to basics, rewarding her for even touching the dumbbell with her nose. She got there eventually, though.

"I am now training Rudy, and I have learned from my experiences with Chips. Rudy has been trained properly, using positive reinforcement methods, from day one. He has also received a heavy dose of early attention training. Results so far have been superb. At eight months old, I can see already that he has the potential to go far beyond Chips in the Obedience arena.

AGILITY

Agility is best described as an obstacle course for dogs, which must be completed as quickly and as accurately as possible. It is great fun for dogs and owners alike. Beagles have acquitted themselves very well in this sport, and, if you are interested in trying it, some tips are given below. However, it is recommended that you join an Agility training club, where expert instructors will be on hand to teach you and your dog how to negotiate the obstacles safely. Your national kennel club will be able to provide you with details.

Age concern and fitness

Agility is a demanding sport, so puppies and growing dogs must not compete in case they damage their delicate joints and ligaments. Most kennel clubs impose an age limit of between one year and 18 months before a dog is permitted to

enter Agility competitions. Even more important, remember that no dog under this age should be encouraged to jump, even at home, no matter how much they seem to enjoy it.

Once your Beagle is old enough to try Agility, you will need to make sure that he is fit enough to take part. Due to his working heritage, the Beagle requires a sensible amount of exercise on a daily basis, so, in most cases, your dog should be more than equal to the challenge. You, however, may not be. The speed at which some dogs tackle an Agility course is phenomenal, and you will need to make sure that you can keep up with your Beagle!

The obstacles

There are numerous obstacles, which include:
• A dog walk (a narrow, elevated walkway with a ramp at either end)

- A long or broad jump
- A seesaw or teeter-totter
- An A-frame (a steep, A-shaped ramp)
- Hurdles
- Poles, which the dog must weave through
- Tunnels and chutes

For each obstacle, you will need a command that tells your Beagle he is to tackle it. Most trainers use the "say it as the dog does it" approach for teaching commands. In other words, say *"Tunnel"* as your dog runs through it. If you do this often enough, your Beagle will soon learn to associate the command with his actions. It is essential that you use the commands consistently. If you choose the

command *"Jump"* for the long jump, don't intersperse it with *"Over,"* or you will confuse your dog. The most commonly used commands are as follows:

Equipment	Command
Hurdles	Over
Long jump	Jump
Tire	Tire
Weave poles	Weave
Dog walk	Walk
A-frame	Ramp
Seesaw	Seesaw
Tunnel	Tunnel

SYDNEY'S SASSY LITTLE BIT

Sydney Armstrong, from Raleigh, North Carolina, takes part in Agility with her nine-year-old Beagle Agility star, Sassy (UACH Sydney's Sassy Little Bit NA, NAJ, NAP, OAP, NJP, NAC-V, OJC-V, CGC).

"I've always had a Beagle in my pack for the last 25 years. I love the breed—sweet, independent, and, in my opinion, wonderful dogs and companions. When I discovered Agility, I definitely wanted to participate with the breed I love. A previous Beagle I had was very shy and skittish around people, and I wanted to make sure that this didn't happen with Sassy. So, I joined a training class that did both Agility and Obedience. We quickly found that we both

loved Agility, and I can think of no more fun than doing Agility with the breed I love.

"Sassy took to Agility like a duck to water. She learned the contact obstacles, the jumps and the distance running in no time, but the weave poles presented a bit more of a problem. Sassy doesn't like them; they're the hardest obstacle for her. I'd like to do more training with her, but I have only a small yard, so we are limited to Agility training twice a week at our class. It's amazing how far Sassy has come just from this!

"To begin with, I never thought I'd compete with Sassy; I thought we'd just have a bit of fun. However, we were definitely bitten by the bug! I am so proud of her when she reaches the top of her classes. She needs just two more qualifying runs to earn her Agility Champion Excellent title, one of the highest titles awarded by the United Kennel Club in the UK. I'm hoping that this will happen by fall. She is also competing at the Excellent level in AKC Agility, and at the Elite level for jumpers for NADAC.

"What makes Sassy's achievements even more special is that she will compete at this level with a different handler. I have a bad knee and can no longer keep up with Sassy, so a friend of mine has been running with her for the last year or so. The first time we tried this, it didn't go too well. My friend let Sassy off her leash and she promptly turned tail and left the ring without tackling a single obstacle! She's come a long way since then, and now she runs without me with no problems at all. While I'd love to be the one out there running with my dog, it makes me so proud to see that she goes out, runs so well with my friend, and that she enjoys the sport so much. Of course, I also love the fact that, when she finishes, she immediately looks for me and comes running to me.

"From my experiences, I think Beagles are definitely well suited to Agility, although it's not appropriate for all. I have another Beagle, Snickers, who doesn't like Agility. She'll do it, and I think if she enjoyed it she would be really good at it; she's so athletic. But, she doesn't like it and it wouldn't be fair to force her. Sassy, on the other hand, can't get enough. She is typical of most Beagles, and we have the occasional problem when her nose gets the better of her, but, as a general rule, she simply loves the sport. I think most Beagles would."

Sassy learned to jump in no time.

Teaching the weaves was quite a challenge.

Sassy tackles the A-frame.

FLYBALL

Flyball is a relay race for dogs, in which two competing teams of four dogs race against each other. A dog is released from the starting line, and has to run to the other end of the track, jumping over four hurdles on the way. At the end of the track is a Flyball box, which the dog must trigger to release a tennis ball. The dog catches the ball and then races back over the four hurdles to the starting line. As soon as the dog crosses the line, the second dog is released, and so on. The winning team is the one in which all four dogs have successfully completed their run in the fastest time.

Flyball is relatively easy to learn and it is enormous fun. Your national kennel club will be able to let you know about clubs in your area, and with Flyball becoming an increasingly popular sport, the number of clubs is growing all the time.

DAZEY THE DOGGED

Lisa Yeowell from Alton, Ontario, Canada, has kept dogs for years. After acquiring a German Shepherd Dog that was "starved for attention," she decided that her newfound canine friend needed something to do that was fun and one-on-one. So began a love affair with Flyball, and the rest, as they say, is history.

"I am very fortunate to be living where I am. Southern Ontario is one of the densest regions in North America for Flyballers. Finding a really good club virtually on my doorstep wasn't difficult.

"My German Shepherd Dog, Chinook, took so well to Flyball that I've been involved with it ever since. I have trained all of the other five dogs I've had to play Flyball, including an American Foxhound, so, when I got my Beagle, Dazey, in 1998, it was only natural that she'd try it too.

"Dazey is my first Beagle, so I don't know how typical of the breed she is. However, I know from experience, particularly with my American Foxhound, that training a scenthound to do Flyball is often quite difficult—they are distracted by smells so easily. Beagles can also be incredibly stubborn, and if there is any food nearby, training goes out the window! However, you can turn this obsession with food to your advantage; most Beagles will be extremely motivated by offerings of treats for doing what is asked of them in a training class. You have to be patient though. It is important for scenthound owners to remember that, by asking your dog to bring a lifeless, boring tennis ball back to you, you are fighting nearly 1,000 years of instinct. However, it certainly helps that Beagles are very loveable and willing to please.

"The first step when training any dog for Flyball is to find a really good motivator, usually food, as I said. You need to work on getting a solid Recall, first on flat land, without any obstacles, and then, eventually, over the jumps. Next, the dog has to learn how to correctly turn on the box. Most dogs learn how to turn without any problem, but it is important that they learn how to do it correctly.

This is because the proper technique is far less demanding on the dog's joints. A dog that runs at full speed, slams into the box, turns, and then scrambles back is placing a lot of strain on his joints.

"Once your dog has mastered the Recall over the jumps, including how to turn on the box, the next step it to teach him how to retrieve a tennis ball. Then he has to learn how to pass by other dogs, because when they are running a race, the dogs will have to cross each other at full speed. Once all the various elements have been thoroughly learned, the final step is to put it all together, and then you're playing Flyball.

Lisa sets Dazey up at the start of a run.

"Despite the problems of training a scenthound, Dazey has turned out to be one of my easier ventures in Flyball training so far. She has occasionally fumbled the ball while at the box, and the ball has bounced out of the ring, but while most dogs would just turn around and come back, Dazey would follow the ball almost out of the building. Thirty seconds later, she would return with the ball in her mouth and continue back over the jumps. I remember one occasion when she did this—the crowd really cheered!

Dazey sets off at speed.

"Dazey really loves Flyball. She's quite experienced now, and she has such a happy-go-lucky attitude that she'll even run with one of my teammates if I can't be at a tournament. At one point, she was the number two Beagle in North America, although circumstances have meant she's slipped down the rankings a bit recently. However, we are now back on track and hopefully she'll get back to number two, or even number one! She now merits her FMX (Flyball Master Excellent), the third-highest award a Flyball dog can get. I am so proud of her."

Working the Flyball box.

WORKING BEAGLES

There are many packs of working Beagles both in the United States and the UK, hunting hare or rabbit, or participating in drag hunting (where the dogs follow the trail of an artificial scent—see below). Beagles love to use their noses; it is, after all, exactly what they have been bred for.

If you are interested in finding out more, your breed club will be able to provide you with further details. In the UK, The Beagle Club has a special section devoted to working activities and Field Trials, while in America, the National Beagle Club offers a similar service.

Beagling

The hunting of hare on foot with a pack of Beagles is one of the oldest of working-Beagle sports. It is believed to have existed in England as early as 1400 A.D., although the hounds concerned would not have been recognizable as the modern-day Beagle.

Since then, the sport has experienced highs and lows of popularity, although it is a relatively strong sport today. If you are interested in finding out more, your breed club (or an Internet search engine) will give you details about groups in your area.

Field Trials

Field Trials have developed to test the working ability of hunting dogs in competitive conditions. They are very popular, attracting many competitors and spectators. If you love to see dogs working as they were intended to, this sport may be exactly what you are looking for.

In the United States, the AKC holds dedicated Beagle Field Trials, in which Beagles hunt rabbit or hare. In the UK, it is a little more confusing. Beagle Field Trials are not the same as Kennel Club Field Trials. The latter is open to several breeds, and tests a dog's ability with a variety of game and in a diverse range of situations. Dogs entering these trials need to stay calm around gunfire. Beagle Field Trials are hosted by The Beagle Club, and they do not work with live game.

Drag hunting

Drag hunting is a popular sport on both sides of the Atlantic, although probably more so in the UK. Hunting is currently a highly controversial political issue in the UK, with the opposing camps deeply polarized. While the sport is yet to be banned, drag hunting is the ideal solution for those who are uncomfortable with the idea of hunting live quarry but who want to encourage their Beagle's natural instincts.

The drag-hunting season normally lasts from September to March. Meetings are held at various venues, and drags are run over many different types of countryside, from hilly arable land to lowland pastures. The Beagles follow an artificial scent laid earlier. This normally involves soaking a length of towel or absorbent cloth in a scent and dragging the cloth on the end of a rope to create a trail. Today, special purposely produced scents are available for drag hunting, although most meets use a mixture of aniseed oil and vegetable cooking oil.

BONNIE BEAGLING

David Nicholson, from Yorkshire, England, acquired his first Beagle in 1962. Since then, he has worked as a puppy walker, preparing Beagle puppies for working life, as well as participating in the sport himself.

"My first Beagle, Bonnie (Bangle of Bardenford), was given to me for my 14th birthday. She was destructive, greedy, and a great escapologist, but I loved her dearly. At five months of age, she celebrated her first Christmas in style by opening the oven door, dragging the turkey into the middle of the kitchen floor, and gorging herself!

"Like all Beagles, Bonnie loved her walks in the surrounding countryside. At that time, I lived in the middle of Derbyshire, so we were lucky to have a wide variety of walks—moorland, woods, fields, and the banks of the River Derwent. Naturally, we encountered quite a range of wildlife while we were enjoying our jaunts, and it soon became apparent that Bonnie had a strong hunting instinct. She would frequently put up pheasant, hare, and rabbit. During the winters of the mid-1960s, we had some heavy snowfall and it was fascinating to watch Bonnie, nose down, stern wagging, in full cry, following the tracks of a deer or a rabbit.

"I think it was Bonnie's interest in hunting that sparked off mine, although it was several years later before I was able to become involved with the working side of the breed. By the mid-1980s I had moved to West Yorkshire and established my own line of show Beagles under the Sabinhay suffix. I had made friends with some enthusiastic hunting people and it seemed inevitable that I should become involved with Beagling. There are two well-known Beagling packs close by, the Colne Valley Beagles and the Holme Valley Beagles. I followed the Colne Valley Beagles and then became involved in puppy walking.

Holme Valley Henna, worked by David Nicholson, puppy show winner.

"Puppy walking is a long-standing tradition in packs of hunting hounds. It is a way of socializing young hounds before they join their pack to get on with the serious business of hunting. The puppy walker keeps the puppies for several months, acquainting them with as many different sights and sounds of the countryside as possible, and returns them toward the end of the hunting season, in February or March. In all, I've walked more than 30 puppies over the past 20 years for the Colne Valley and the Holme Valley packs.

"Seeing a puppy you have walked go on to become a successful hunting hound is extremely rewarding. Each year, the hunt holds its annual puppy show, where the newly socialized pups are exhibited and judged by two

Continued overleaf

"There is no greater joy than watching hounds work."

guest judges, one of whom is usually a Master of Hounds. After the young puppies have been judged, a trophy is awarded to the youngster that has proven himself and excelled at his first year of working in the field. It is a great honor to win this award, and when one of the dogs you've walked wins, it is a wonderful feeling.

"Hunting hounds are delightful to be with, and usually very obedient. That said, I remember one occasion at a Holme Valley Beagles show when the hounds caused a riot. At the show, tea and refreshments are served, often in a tent. The refreshments are strictly for members of the hunt and their guests, but on this occasion the hounds had other ideas and stormed the tent for their share of the goodies. After much shouting and shooing, and a few stolen sandwiches, the riot was quashed and the hounds were eventually kennelled—much to their disgust!

COUNTRY WALKS

"From May to September, I am involved in exercising the Holme Valley Beagles. It is a way of keeping them fit and disciplined, as well as introducing younger members of the pack. Some of the older hounds are coupled to the youngsters that have just returned from puppy walking with specially made pairs of collars linked to each other by short chains. These 'couplings' are removed once the youngsters have learned to stay with the pack. It is a great opportunity to see the hounds develop as a pack, and I've seen many Beagles mature into fantastic working dogs as adults.

"Among my favorites are two that I have walked for the Colne Valley Beagles. They were litter sisters, Fickle and Famous. Famous was a little beauty and won several awards. Fickle, while not as pretty as her sister, proved to be one of the best workers in the pack. Another favorite of mine, from the Holme Valley pack, was Amber, whom I whelped in my own kennels. She was liver-tan and white, a color unacceptable to the show scene, and largely ignored by working groups. Amber proved herself to be one of the best workers for the Holme Valley, although she

The Holme Valley Beagles at exercise with huntsman David Clarke.

was the smallest in the pack, being 14 inches (36 cm) at the shoulder. After a brilliant working record covering eight seasons, she eventually retired when she was beginning to find the challenges of high stone walls, steep valley sides, and thick heather a little too rigorous.

WORKING LEGACY
"After all the hard work involved in training puppies, it is delightful to keep in touch with their progress and see them working in the field. There is no greater joy than watching hounds work, streaming in full cry across rugged moorland, negotiating stone walls, or checking to find that elusive scent of the quarry, noses to the ground, sterns wagging urgently, performing the job that they and their ancestors have done for centuries."

Several trails may be laid, ranging between half a mile and 2 miles (1 and 3 km), so the ideal drag hunt area needs to be approximately 300 acres (125 ha) to allow for this. The trail should test the Beagle's abilities in a range of settings, so it should go over undulating ground and include streams and hedges.

The hounds gather at the start of the trail and are released on the instruction of the Field Master, usually by a blast on a whistle or a horn. Normally, hounds are released in two groups, the first comprising proven working hounds, and the latter consisting of novices. The idea behind this is that the novices will follow the proven workers and so, hopefully, get the idea of what it's all about.

DIY drag hunting
If drag hunting appeals to you, why not follow the advice of retired Field Master Neill Hannon? If you and your Beagle enjoy practicing the following tips, contact your national Beagle club to find out more.

"It is best to begin training in your backyard, but once your hound has grasped the idea, you can progress to local fields or parks. You may feel very silly running around a park, towing a length or cord with an old rag attached, but you'd be amazed at how many people will stop and take an interest!

"To scent the rag, you will need aniseed oil. This can be difficult to obtain and very expensive, but you can make your own substitute by boiling aniseed candies or aniseed-flavored dog chews to make a weak liquid that can be mixed with vegetable oil. Alternatively, you could try asking at a pharmacy. You'd be surprised at how many pharmacists can be persuaded once they know the highly unusual reason for the request!

"To begin with, lay short lines, and keep some of your Beagle's favorite treats at the end of the trail. Walk your hound along the line you have laid, encouraging him to 'Find it.' He will soon get the idea that following the line results in his getting a tasty reward. A word of warning, however: Don't finish your trail in the same place every time. Beagles are notoriously clever and will soon work out that there is a quicker way to get the treats."

The pack at full cry, thoroughly enjoying the sport of drag hunting.

Mitchell and Lisa Read, from Essex, England, got their first Beagle, Innkeeper Dialynne (or Inky for short), three years ago, and soon became involved in drag hunting.

"A short time after we got Inky, the owners of his litter sister asked us if we'd like to go to a drag hunt. We were hooked from the start!

"Inky absolutely loves drag hunting. Beagles have been bred to work and they have an incredible amount of energy. Drag hunting is an ideal way of utilizing the dog's natural instincts and using up all that energy. Inky covers about 6 to 7 miles (11–12 km) on an average hunt.

"The dogs also seem to love the pack element of the hunt. By nature, dogs are pack animals, but most of us don't keep our dogs in a pack setting. At a drag hunt, it doesn't matter how many dogs are gathered; as soon as they are released on the trail, it's as if they become one. In fact, it's so hard to distinguish the dogs from each other that some owners have special jackets for their dogs so that they can identify them from a distance.

"The average hunt lasts about three hours or so. The Field Master blows two whistles to begin; the first whistle allows the more experienced, qualified dogs to go, while the second whistle allows the remainder to shoot off on the trail. The sight of all those Beagles lined up at the start, waiting for the whistle to blow, is one of the things I love most about drag hunting. You have to see it—and hear it— to believe it! The noise is incredible! Every dog is barking and baying and creating a racket in their excitement to begin the chase. Then, when the whistle finally blows, they're off, and all you can see is up to 40 Beagle behinds running away from you.

"We'd recommend drag hunting to anyone committed to getting the best from his Beagle. You don't need to be experienced or qualified to go along. Inky had never done anything like this before his first hunt, but he took to it right away. Instinct took over and he seemed to know just what to do. Occasionally, inexperienced dogs can become distracted by a 'real' scent, such as a fox in a neighboring field, but they all come in eventually. Our best achievement with Inky was when he came in fourth, after following a line perfectly.

"Drag hunting is an excellent way of socializing your Beagle with other dogs, and it's also a great way of socializing yourself! We usually have a meal and a few drinks with other enthusiasts on the day of the hunt. Everyone is made to feel at home, whether they come from a traditional rural background or they are city-dwellers like us looking for a novel way to get out into the country with their dog."

THE FIELD MASTER

Neill and Mary Hannon of Suffolk, England, got their first Beagle in 1962. They currently have four hounds: eight-year-old Tilly (Lunar Mist from Bondlea); two of her progeny, Bellamy (Aldemarsh Bellamy) and Dotty (Aldemarsh Milkmaid), both aged four; and Bellamy's son, Merlin (Hendol Dragon at Aldemarsh), aged 16 months. Neill has been Field Master for the Working Section of The Beagle Club for 11 years.

"We started drag hunting in 1983, when we found that our Beagle was capable of following a boot trail run by our children. In 1985, we obtained a puppy, Bill (Valedown Minstrel Boy), who showed every sign of being a good hunter. In the 14 years we had Bill, he won 12 Working Certificates (a record number) and he was awarded Best Novice, Best Hound, and Best Veteran. Those were very happy years.

"At around the same time as I got Bill, I took on Field Mastership of the Working Section of The Beagle Club. Although this was quite demanding, it was thoroughly enjoyable. Part of my job was to oversee a day's 'meet' and to release the hounds at the start. There's nothing quite like seeing a pack of Beagles assembled at the start of a drag trail. I also got the chance to see a lot of hounds and to assess their skills.

"At the end of the drag-hunting season, Field Trials are held. These offer the opportunity to present the hounds that have participated in the season's meets for the assessment of two invited Masters of Hounds. These judges have extensive experience watching hounds hunting and are

Continued overleaf

Club members and Beagles waiting for the course to be laid.

> ❝ **You get really hooked on enjoying the sight of the hounds in the field.** ❞

able to assess the manner in which our hounds are capable of working. Hounds that really hunt always 'give tongue' (that is, they make a sound that's impossible to describe accurately, but is a little like yodeling) in pursuit of their quarry. This is one of the characteristics that the judges will seek. It is great to see owners who can normally be heard telling their Beagles to stop barking taking so much enjoyment from the 'music' of hounds in the field. For once, the

Picking up the trail—and then off in hot pursuit.

owners find it a really cheering sound.

"One of the other nice aspects to Field Trials is that, after the main event, a truly splendid luncheon is organized, at which the judges deliver their verdicts and present the awards. It is a very social occasion and one that everyone enjoys.

"In my mind, drag hunting and Field Trials are addictive, you get really hooked on enjoying the sight of hounds in the field, doing exactly what they were bred for."

THERAPY DOGS

Imagine how bereft your life would seem without your Beagle. Think of sunlit walks, the hugs, and the love that you would miss. Sadly, many people are in this situation. A dog-loving elderly couple may have had to give up their beloved dog if they are no longer fit enough to walk him. Think of those in nursing homes, children's homes, hospitals, and such.

You may have already heard of therapy dogs. They have become more high profile in recent years, as research has demonstrated how petting an animal can lower stress, reduce blood pressure, relieve anxiety, and boost the immune system. This is not to mention the sheer

pleasure that a person can get from animal companionship. All therapy dogs must have proven, trustworthy characters before they are allowed to "go to work," and they do an enormous amount of good.

Anyone with the right type of dog can get involved. If your Beagle has an affectionate personality, and he is calm in new environments, he could make an ideal therapy dog. Not only will he love the work, but you, too, will derive enormous satisfaction from the amount of good that you are doing for others less fortunate than yourself. Your national kennel club can provide you with the details of the main therapy dog organizations in your area.

GENEROUS GABBY

Tara Mann from Durham, North Carolina, has been doing therapy work with her Beagle, Gabby, for about two years. Gabby is a rescued dog, but, with Tara's help, she is now doing a bit of rescuing herself.

"I already had a Beagle when I got Gabby. I love the breed, although I don't think they're for everyone—they need a lot of work and a lot of love. There is an enormous range of temperaments within the breed. Gabby is a couch potato and sleeps most of the day, but my other Beagle, Murphy, who is the same age, is very active and into everything.

PUPPY LOVE
"I acquired Gabby when I applied to adopt her from Triangle Beagle Rescue. She was found as a stray puppy, spayed and vaccinated, and then placed for adoption. Once I had passed the approval procedures, she was all mine, and I've loved her ever since.

"Once I got Gabby, I enrolled her in training classes. One of the women attending the class knew about therapy work and told me all about it. It really piqued my interest and I decided to find out more. After doing some research, I thought that Gabby had the perfect temperament for it; she loves nothing more than to curl up tight right beside me and get lots of love.

"I got in touch with a registered therapy organization, the Delta Society, and attended a training class to prepare us for the exam. The exam has two parts—a skills test and an aptitude test. The skills test shows the evaluator that you can control your dog and that she can follow basic commands, while the aptitude test simulates conditions that we may encounter,

such as clumsy petting, wheelchairs or other medical equipment, and several 'stressors'—to see how the dog reacts under pressure. Gabby passed with flying colors.

"Gabby and I are now regular visitors to the Ronald McDonald House (a home for children and their families who come for surgery or treatment at a nearby hospital), and the Durham Rehabilitation Institute (a center that teaches patients who have suffered amputations, spinal injuries, strokes, or head injuries, to manage their disabilities and live as independently as possible).

"When someone has had a really long, tough day of treatment or physiotherapy, a visit from Gabby really seems to brighten them up. At the rehab center, I remember going to visit a man with a back injury, who had to lie flat on his back. He was eating cheese spread. Gabby climbed on the bed, curled up next to him, and began 'kissing' his hand. I told him that

Continued overleaf

Tara pictured with Gabby.

" Getting involved with therapy work is one of the best things I have ever done!"

cheese was Gabby's favorite treat and he asked if he could give her some. After he had fed her the majority of his cheese and it was time to leave, I had to carry Gabby out, because she wasn't about to leave, she was so hopeful for more cheese. The man thought this was hilarious, and he just laughed and laughed.

"Another time, I used to visit a young girl who was receiving treatment for a brain tumor. She got very excited when Gabby visited, and her mother told us that she was always talking about Gabby. Even when the girl's treatments meant that she couldn't walk anymore, she still had a smile for Gabby and would let her curl up next to her, stroking her for the entire visit. When the girl finished her treatment, we had to give her a photo of Gabby to take home with her.

MUTUAL REWARD

"It's not all one-sided. Gabby gets just as much from the visits as the patients. When I tell her that we are "going for a visit," she gets very excited. She starts wagging her tail, squeals with anticipation, and runs to the door. When it's time to leave, I literally have to pick her up and carry her out of the door. Otherwise, she will sit or lie down and refuse to leave! She absolutely adores the patients.

"Getting involved in therapy work is one of the best things I have ever done, and I'd recommend it to any dog owner who has a dog with the right temperament to try it. There is nothing more touching than seeing a patient's face light up with a smile as you enter the room, no matter what physical or emotional pain he or she may be in."

Gabby working with children at the Ronald McDonald House.

MISTY MOMENTS

Perrystar Victoria at Valedene (affectionately known as Misty) has belonged to Margaret Dix, of Suffolk, UK, for the last seven years. Misty is Margaret's seventh Beagle in 44 years.

"I had a very friendly Beagle named Emma, so I decided to join the Pets As Therapy program to share her with those who could no longer have a pet. I started by contacting a local nursing home and asking them if they would like a canine visitor. They jumped at the chance. Since then, I have also visited a day center for the elderly and a home for the mentally disturbed.

"When I got Misty, I decided that I'd like her to do some therapy work as well. There was no real training involved, but all registered therapy dogs have to undergo an assessment. They must be friendly around people, they must not be frightened by dropped walking aids, etc., they mustn't jump up, and they mustn't snatch food—people do love to give them treats! I think this is one of the reasons why Misty enjoys therapy work so much.

"Most people that Misty and I visit are delighted. Quite a few of the elderly residents used to own dogs and they seem particularly pleased to have the chance to pet Misty. Dogs are great icebreakers—I've lost count of the stories I've been told about long-gone but much-loved pets. Misty just seems to make people open up. Even those who can't see Misty get some benefit. Some of the partially sighted residents just like to stroke her head and feel her long, soft ears.

"There was one lady we used to visit who lived almost entirely in a world of her own. She never spoke or tried to communicate with anyone. However, whenever Misty was around, she would talk to her doggie visitor with no problem. Another lady loved Misty so much that she would draw cartoons of her.

"Therapy work is not for everyone, nor for every dog, but it can be very rewarding and you can give as much or as little time as you like.

"Beagles are real characters, and they are very versatile. They can take any amount of exercise, in any weather, but they are also content to curl up in a nice armchair given the chance. I think this mix of characteristics makes them perfect for therapy work. They are not for the fainthearted, and you need to let them know who's boss, but life is never dull with a Beagle in the house. I couldn't imagine life without one, or two."

Therapy dog Misty with Margaret: The temperament of the dog is of great importance in therapy work.

CHAPTER SEVEN

SEEKING PERFECTION

All recognized purebred dogs have a Breed Standard, devised by each national kennel club, describing the ideal specimen. It outlines how the breed should look, move, and behave.

The Beagle: A solid, compact dog that looks capable of hunting quarry.

This written blueprint is essential, to ensure that the breed does not alter through changing fashions. Breeders use the Standard as a guide, and it is against the Standard that dogs are judged in the show ring.

There is a common misconception among people that dog shows are little more than beauty contests. This is not true. They honor those dogs that most closely resemble the ideal laid out in the Standard, making these animals more sought after for breeding and stud purposes. This is important because it ensures that these top-dog qualities are passed on to the next generation of dogs, and so assures the breed's future.

The Beagle was bred to hunt, and this is reflected in how he is constructed. The following describes the essential points of the American Kennel Club (AKC) and UK Kennel Club (KC) Standards, and explains how they relate to the Beagle's original function as a scenthound.

The Beagle expression is typically gentle and appealing.

BREED STANDARDS

General appearance
The Beagle is a solid, compact dog that looks capable of hunting quarry.

Characteristics
A cheerful dog that hunts by scent, the Beagle needs to be bold, active, intelligent, and determined. Physically, he needs great stamina to hold his own when chasing prey.

Temperament
Hunting dogs work closely with their human handlers, so they must be friendly, confident, and manageable. Beagles are often described as "merry," and they are never happier than when following a scent, which they will pursue actively and boldly.

Head and skull
The Beagle has the typical "hound head," which is fairly long, slightly domed at the top, and quite broad. The stop (the "step," where the skull meets the muzzle, between the eyes) should be well defined.

The correct nose is essential in a scenthound. To enable him to get the most scent, his nose should be broad, with large, open nostrils.

Eyes
Hound eyes are renowned for melting most hearts and the Beagle is no exception. They should be dark brown or hazel, fairly large, and set well apart (ensuring a more extensive field of vision when hunting). The Beagle expression should be gentle and appealing.

Ears
Some dogs, such as Border Collies, rely a great deal on sounds, to hear any lost sheep or long-distance commands from their owner. Beagles rely more on scent than sound, so they do not need erect ears. Instead, their ears are long, pendulous, and close to the cheek (helping them to be deaf to their owners when they want to be!).

Mouth
The jaws should be strong. The AKC Standard requires the jaws to be level, but does not specify the type of bite required. The KC Standard states that a Beagle should have a scissor bite (where the upper teeth closely overlap the lower teeth). Such a bite would have been needed to hold caught prey securely.

Neck

See a Beagle at work and he has his head to the ground; therefore he needs a sufficiently long neck to enable him to scent. The neck is also slightly arched (to enable him to stoop), and should be "clean" (without folds of loose skin).

Forequarters

The forelegs should be straight, and the pasterns (the "wrist" area) should be short. The forequarters should be quite muscular, conveying the sense of a fit, strong, active dog. The shoulders shouldn't be "loaded," or too heavy; so as not to impede the dog when working.

Body

This is the body of a worker. The ribs are well sprung, giving plenty of lung room, the loins are powerful and broad, and the back is short and strong. The topline should be level.

Hindquarters

The thighs are muscular, to give the dog power and stamina when working, and the stifles are well bent. The hocks are firm and should be parallel to each other. These qualities give the dog plenty of propelling power.

The Beagle should be built on working lines, with straight forelegs, a short, strong body, and muscular hindquarters.

Feet

The feet should be round, firm, and well padded. Many working breeds have this type of foot, as it requires less energy to lift than long, hare feet.

Tail

The tail is slightly curved and is covered well with hair. It is set fairly high, and is carried gaily, although it shouldn't curl over the back. A high tail makes the dog visible to his handler in the field.

Gait/movement

The AKC doesn't give any guidance about movement in the breed. However, it is generally accepted that the Beagle should have a long-reaching stride (to cover ground efficiently), with a powerful rear drive. The back should remain level when he moves.

Coat

To allow him to work well in the cold, wind, and rain, the coat should be dense and weatherproof. The KC Standard calls for it to be short in length, whereas the AKC asks for a medium-length coat.

Color

Any recognized hound color is acceptable (although the KC does not allow liver). In the KC Standard, it states that the tip of the stern (tail) should be white.

All the recognized hound colors are acceptable in the show ring.

Size

The KC gives a desirable height range of between 13 inches (33 cm) and 16 inches (40 cm). For the AKC, there are two size classifications: for dogs not exceeding 13 inches (33 cm) in height, and another for those over 13 inches but below 15 inches (37.5 cm).

FAMILY TREES

When you buy a purebred Beagle, you should be given his pedigree. This is a family tree, showing the dog's lineage. Most pedigrees show three generations, but some may show more than this.

Experienced breeders research dogs' pedigrees carefully, assessing which males and females have contributed to producing good stock. If a health problem is uncovered in a certain line, this can often be isolated to particular dogs, too.

By carefully examining your dog's pedigree, you will be able to see which type of breeding has been used:

• Inbreeding, where very close family members are mated, such as father to daughter. (This type of breeding isn't recommended, as it can produce serious health defects. It is used only in exceptional circumstances by the most experienced breeders.)

• Linebreeding, where more distant family members are mated, such as great-uncles to great-nieces.

• Outcrossing, in which distantly related or completely unrelated animals are bred to (for the purpose of introducing desired, new features to an established family).

Linebreeding

Linebreeding is the most common type of breeding. Each breeder has a particular type of dog, in terms of looks and temperament. By using their own dogs in a breeding program, they are assured that the resulting puppies will keep the family resemblance. However, breeders often have to outcross every now and then to prevent their line from becoming "stale" and inbred (see page 96).

Val Davies, who line-bred Ch. Barrvale Quickstep (pictured), says, "Line-breeding is useful in fixing type without the perils of inbreeding. It can improve stock by picking up on qualities from other generations without introducing possibly unwanted and unknown traits from outcrossing."

Ch. Barrvale Quickstep: An example of linebreeding.

Parents	Grandparents	Great-Grandparents	Great-Great-Grandparents
Ch. Dialynne Toliver Of Tragband	Ch. Soloman Of Dialynne	Ch. Dialynne Gamble	Am. Ch. Appeline Validay Happy Feller
			Ch. Dialynne Nettle
		Kittoch Garland	Ch. Beacott Buckthorn
			Kittoch Glittered
	Tragband Sweet Bird Of Youth	Ch. Dialynne Nimrod Of Ramlacin	Ch. Dialynne Blueboy
			Dialynne Kelly Of Cranwood
		Ch. Too Darn Hot For Tragband	Int. Ch. Graadtres Hot Pursuit Of Rossut
			Dicarl Gays The Word Of Araki
Ch. Nivek Madelaine Of Barrvale	Dufosee Furst Edition	Dufosee Avenger	Ch. Dufosee Harris Tweed
			Dufosee Jessica
		Tragband In Favour At Dufosee	Ch. Dufosee Influence
			Ch. Too Darn Hot For Tragband
	Crickhollow Kathys Clown About Nivek	Crickhollow Swansong	Ch. Soloman Of Dialynne
			Dicarl Gays The Word Of Araki
		Tragband Hot Gossip About Crickhollow	Int. Ch. Graadtres Hot Pursuit Of Rossut
			Dicarl Gays The Word Of Araki

Outcrossing

Outcrossing is used with linebreeding. When deciding on a suitable mate for a female, a breeder will assess the female's qualities and faults. Faults shouldn't be doubled up on, and qualities lacking in the female should be found in a stud dog. Simply put, if the female's front is rather narrow, then a male with a good front will be needed. If the breeder's own dogs do not fit the bill, then he or she will assess other lines, to introduce other qualities to their own kennel.

Champion Cliffmere Quadrant (Max—pictured), bred by Wendy and Doug Hall, is essentially an outcross Champion. However,

Ch. Cliffmere Quadrant: The result of outcross breeding.

there are some duplications in the fifth generation (for example, Korwin Tattler appears several times on both sides). As Wendy says, "Dominant males will always pull the papers together if you go back far enough. Looking at the first three generations, it would appear to be an outcross, but as soon as you start on the fifth generation, it starts to pull together."

Parents	Grandparents	Great-Grandparents	Great-Great-Grandparents
Deanery Draper	Ch. Dufosee Influence	Ch. Dufosee Zenith	Ch. Dialynne Gamble
			Ch. Dufosee Bonnie Girl
		Dufosee Katrina	Ch. Wembury Archer
			Ch. Dufosee Bonnie Girl
	Deanery Destiny	Norcis Uri	Ch. Korwin Monitor
			Crestamere Martha
		Ch. Deanery Dandelion	Ch. Korwin Monitor
			Ch. Deanery Dream Girl
Cliffmere Fleur	Ch. Clarino Hawthorn	Pancrest Sirocco	Ch. Korwin Monitor
			Norcis Glory
		Ch. Clarino Buttercup	Redgate Watchful
			Salcin Joyful
	Cliffmere Gypsy	Ch. Newlin Prefect	Ch. Korwin Monitor
			Newlin Nutmeg
		Crestamere Flower By Cliffmere	Ch. Crestamere Ruler
			Crestamere Tartan Lass

SHOWING

If you are fortunate to own a Beagle that has all the qualities outlined in the Breed Standard (ask the honest advice of the dog's breeder), then you may want to think about exhibiting your dog. Showing is great fun and a good way of becoming more involved with the breed.

If you decide to take up showing your Beagle, you will need to make sure that he is well behaved in the show ring. Ring-training classes help to teach a Beagle what to expect when being shown, from being inspected by a judge and gaiting, to ignoring the other dogs in the lineup. Your breed club or kennel club should be able to give you details of your nearest ring-training class.

Costs

For all its fun, showing is hard work. The cost of traveling around the country, with dogs and equipment in tow, can be considerable. Entry fees can also be costly.

Competition at shows can be extremely fierce, and if you are to stand any chance of success, you will need to spend a great deal of time making sure that your Beagle is in the peak of physical condition.

Tips for success

- Visit as many shows as you can and speak to as many Beagle breeders and enthusiasts as you can. You'll be amazed at what you can learn.
- Join a breed club and attend its seminars.
- Go to ring-training classes.

- Remember that success won't happen overnight. It takes time, money, patience, and hard work to achieve success—and, of course, the right dog!
- Most important of all, remember that your Beagle is special. He should be treated as a much-loved pet first and foremost, and as a show dog second. Even if he fails to place, he should remain the most special dog in the world to you.

Showing is highly competitive at the top level.

FROM PUPPY TO CHAMPION

Ch. Donay Kappa (aka Gus)

Pat and Keith Hills' Ch. Donay Kappa (pet name: Gus), got his first Challenge Certificate (CC) as a junior, and was made up, with his third CC, at the age of three years. Currently he has five CCs and seven Reserve CCs. Gus was in the second litter that the Hills bred. Pat says, "As you can imagine, I am very proud of him. We have had a lot of fun, and he is a true showman." Here, he is pictured from the age of two weeks to three years, showing how he has developed from a cute puppy into a complete showstopper.

The litter pictured at two weeks: Gus is third from right.

At four weeks: Gus is pictured left.

At 12 weeks: Gus is in the middle.

At 16 weeks: Gus in his pen.

Gus aged two-
and-a-half years.

Ch. Donay Kappa,
pictured at three, soon
after winning his title.

PANDEMONIUM PEBBLES

arion Hunt from Hampshire, England, is an enthusiastic Beagle handler. Originally a Chihuahua fan, her husband's love of Beagles began a devotion to the breed that, for Marion, has lasted for three decades.

"Over the last 30 years, I have shown about 15 of my own dogs as well as a few for other people. I decided to take up showing because the camaraderie of the show world appealed to me, and I also liked the competition side of things.

"I started off by showing one or two of my Chihuahuas, but quickly changed to showing Beagles instead. When my husband decided that he'd like what he joked was 'a real dog' and mentioned Beagles in particular, I decided to take him up on the suggestion. We've never looked back since!

"Our first Beagle was Sonnet of Bondlea, or Tangle as we called her for short. I showed her a little and she won a few cards (the UK equivalent of American ribbons), but this was still quite early on in our show career.

Ch. & Ir. Ch. Valsacre Tactful Of Bondlea winning Best of Breed at Crufts, Dog Show, UK.

"There's such excitement when you're in the ring with a Beagle you have helped to make into a Champion."

EARLY DAYS

"I remember one of my first shows, when I was still learning the ropes. I had taken a book about showing dogs along with me, hoping I could glean something from it that would make the day a success. Needless to say, I didn't achieve much that day, and I felt somewhat silly afterward, but it was a valuable learning experience. It is important to go to a show prepared!

"I've had some hair-raising experiences too! At one show, I was entering my Beagle Pebbles, but she managed to slip her leash and wander up the nearby highway! Fortunately, she lived to tell the tale, making it to the grand old age of 16.

VALUABLE EXPERIENCE

"The great thing about showing Beagles is that you can be involved as little or as much as you like. Over the years, I've learned to take things at a steady pace, and I'd advise anyone thinking of taking up showing to learn from experience.

"Don't take things too seriously, be prepared to work hard, and don't expect too much at the beginning. It takes experience, a great dog, and a fair amount of luck for success to happen, and that takes time. You have to start at the bottom and work up.

"Go to a few shows to watch and learn the ropes. Enter some small shows until you are familiar with the way it all works. And then, see how far you can go.

"You also have to find something that will convince your Beagle to stand still in the show ring—not the easiest of tasks! I've had some battles with mine, but fortunately, I've found that food tends to work quite well. It's well worth thinking about ring-training classes as well, where you can learn a lot about how to present your dog and yourself to the best advantage.

REAPING THE REWARDS

"Since those early days, I have had four Champions, three of which are Beagles.

"My first Champion was Ch. Bondlea Poet, shortly followed by UK and Irish Ch. Bondlea Pebbles (the one that went up the highway), and UK and Irish Ch. Valsacre Tactful of Bondlea—a Crufts Best Of Breed winner—who I partly own with Jo Norris.

"There is such excitement and a sense of achievement when you're in the ring with a Beagle that you have just helped to make into a Champion. The days spent in a muddy field in the wet weather, and all the hard work that goes into getting ready for a show, are all forgotten."

CHAPTER EIGHT

HEALTH CARE

Amiable and alert, Beagles are naturally long-lived and particularly hardy. Couple this with a short coat, and the result is virtually the perfect companion for an active household.

After more than 40 years of a busy veterinary practice, I regard the Beagle as a relatively trouble-free dog. However, that is not to say that problems do not arise. There are a few breed-specific conditions about which owners or intending owners should be aware, but these, compared with other popular breeds, are relatively few. These problems are explained individually later in the chapter.

PREVENTIVE CARE

Regardless of the breed, size, sex, or age of the pet, mention preventive care to any dog owner and the response invariably concerns vaccination, fleas, and worms. In fact, it involves much more than this.

OBESITY AND DIET

Breed Standards on both sides of the Atlantic emphasize the athleticism of the Beagle. Details need not concern us here, but the result is a dog bouncing with energy and needing adequate exercise on a daily basis. Reduced exercise does not result in a diminished appetite in Beagles, as with some breeds. It is one of the sad facts of life that middle-aged, obese Beagles are a common sight in veterinary practice. Therefore, exercise and a well-balanced, carefully controlled diet are essential parts of preventive care.

A Beagle puppy will soon become established as a member of the family, but we should remember that dogs are not people, even though sometimes they act like us. We thrive on variety in our diet. If we introduce too much variety into our Beagle's diet, regardless of the amount of exercise we are trying to provide, we will end up with a rather portly pet.

Start off as you plan to continue! In my experience, most Beagles will eat virtually

Exercise and a well-balanced diet are vital components in preventing obesity.

anything, so provide a balanced diet right from the beginning, day in, day out, year in, year out. Change it only if health problems dictate that you should, or if your Beagle suddenly starts to refuse the food. Should this happen, it is worth consulting your veterinarian.

By far the easiest way to provide this balanced complete diet is to feed one of the commercial brands of dog food. A great variety is available in all supermarkets, and advice from the breeder and from your veterinarian is worthwhile regarding choice.

Contrary to popular belief, many of the bowel upsets seen in practice are not the result of infections and bugs, but simply due to being given highly delectable but nonetheless unfamiliar foods. Some turkey at Christmas or Thanksgiving can spell disaster when your dog

is used to a commercially produced complete diet. That nice bit of fatty meat bought as a special treat on his birthday can end up being expensive if it results in several trips to the veterinarian because of the ensuing diarrhea!

For more information about diet, see Chapter Five.

ABOUT SUPPLEMENTS

Once you have selected a complete, balanced diet, there may be no need to give supplements. Balanced complete diets do not need the addition of extra vitamins, minerals, or other supplements. It has been shown that the addition of minerals, particularly calcium and phosphorus, can be harmful.

EXERCISE

Regular exercise has to be considered as part of preventive care. Remember, Beagles have a long history of chasing hares, rabbits, and other small game, hour after hour. That is certainly not for sedentary types. They need rather more than a walk around the block on a leash, whatever the weather.

However, while immature, too much exercise can actually be deleterious and result in joint and bone problems.

Despite all our efforts at diet control, some Beagles, like some people, tend to put on weight as they grow older. Remember that these dogs still require regular exercise, although clearly it has to be tailored to the individual dog or the problem. Often this will result in reducing the distance and increasing the number of outings. Also, overweight dogs should not be exercised in very hot weather, as heatstroke could occur.

Dogs age just as we do, but unfortunately they do it more quickly. If your dog seems to be slowing down rapidly, consult your veterinarian. A checkup is indicated in such cases.

VACCINATIONS

In this section the terms "vaccination" and "inoculation" are used synonymously, although there are subtle differences.

Vaccination stimulates the subject to produce immunity against the disease without developing symptoms of the disease. The vaccine need not be directly introduced into the tissues of the body. For example, vaccination against kennel cough can be achieved by instilling a few drops up the nose.

Inoculation means introducing an agent into the tissues of the body to stimulate an immune response. This usually involves an injection, although human smallpox vaccine, for example, is introduced by scarifying the skin of the arm and not by injection.

Vaccination stimulates your Beagle to produce an active immunity against one or, as is more common today, a collection of infectious

A sedentary lifestyle will not suit the Beagle, which was bred to chase game for many hours.

The use of vaccines has transformed the fight against disease.

diseases caused by microorganisms. Animals, including us, develop a natural immunity to certain diseases as a result of being exposed to the germs. If these germs do not replicate (reproduce) quickly enough to overcome our natural defenses, they are expelled from the body, leaving behind a legacy in the form of stronger defenses. This is immunity. Then, if the body is exposed to the same organism on future occasions, it will be expelled even quicker without any signs of illness. At the same time, the "acquired immunity" is reinforced each time.

If the germ is very powerful, it can quickly overcome the body's natural defenses. Before vaccination, distemper in dogs was an example of a virus so powerful that usually the body's resistance was ineffective and death resulted.

It is one of the milestones of medical history that it was learned that by weakening the micro-organism, it would not cause disease but still stimulated the body to produce immunity.

Vaccines are produced by a variety of methods. In some vaccines, the causal agent has been killed, so that it is harmless and cannot cause the disease but can still stimulate an immunity. These are inactivated vaccines (also known as "killed vaccines").

In others the causal organism is weakened by various means so that it is no longer a disease producer (or occasionally produces only very mild signs), but still stimulates the body to produce a strong immunity. These are known as attenuated vaccines.

To complicate the vaccination story further, several components may be incorporated into one vaccine, so that immunity can be provided against a number of diseases with just one or two simple injections. This is known as active immunity.

Puppy immunity

All animals acquire some immunity from the mother while in the uterus. After birth, that immunity is boosted (increased) all the time the puppy suckles the first milk (colostrum). This is called passive immunity.

Once weaning takes place, this immune resistance is no longer being reinforced and soon fades. In the days before vaccination was common, this was the time when puppies were most vulnerable. It was also the time when they were meeting all the challenges of life.

Consequently, they frequently died (for example, from distemper or hepatitis) before they ever became fully grown. In those days, if a puppy was lucky enough to survive the initial infection, the acquired immunity was boosted every time the puppy came into contact with dogs, or where dogs had been, because the diseases were so common.

Active immunity, just like passive immunity acquired by the puppy from the mother, does not last forever. Protection can last just a few months, as in the case of tracheobronchitis (kennel cough), or years (for example, distemper or canine adenovirus/hepatitis).

Today, largely as the result of vaccination, many serious canine killer diseases are no longer prevalent and therefore, natural challenge (boosting) does not occur. Therefore, as part of the vaccination program, regular booster shots should be considered essential.

Primary vaccination

Primary vaccination should be started as soon as the passive immunity acquired from the female has declined sufficiently to allow the puppy to develop a protective active immunity. If vaccinated too early, circulating maternal antibodies will destroy the vaccine before an immune response has developed and no protection is built up. When the passive immunity has disappeared completely, the puppy is totally unprotected, although you, and often your veterinarian, may think all is well since the shots have been given.

It is possible to tell precisely the best time to vaccinate the puppy to ensure that as effective an immunity as possible is built up and also to ascertain whether the immune response achieved is high enough to be protective. The problem is that this involves blood tests, the cost for which is sometimes considerably greater than the total

When puppies are weaned, their immunity starts to fade.

cost of the vaccination. In addition, there is stress to the puppy, since repeated blood samples have to be taken. Consequently, manufacturers have worked to develop vaccines that will stimulate the puppy to build up a solid, active immunity, even in the face of some circulating maternal antibodies.

This has been a major breakthrough, since it means that puppies can be vaccinated early enough that they have an active immunity by 10 to 12 weeks of age; socialization and training can start, therefore, while the puppy is at a receptive stage. This ensures that you have a well-trained and biddable Beagle with a minimum of effort.

Puppies can be vaccinated earlier, which means that training and socialization can get underway.

Having accepted that vaccination does not last forever and that booster shots are necessary, the problem is: when and how frequently? In the past, veterinarians have recommended routine annual booster shots. For the last few years, however, there have been mounting concerns regarding the possibility of some dogs developing reactions to booster shots. This has led to a radical reassessment.

Polyvalent vaccines

Polyvalent (multivalent) vaccines give protection against a collection of diseases. They are very popular since they are economical; they cost considerably less in terms of cash, time, and stress than the separate injections against each of the inoculable diseases.

Before any such vaccine can be marketed, it must receive a product license from the appropriate government body, and evidence has to be submitted regarding how effective they are, and how long they last, relating to the immunity conferred by the shortest-acting component. This is reflected in the product license upon which the manufacturers' recommendations are based. Hence, multivalent vaccines became saddled with the annual booster shots recommendation despite the fact that it was discovered that some components, such as canine adenovirus/hepatitis, confer at least a two-year immunity and possibly longer.

Adverse reactions

Over the last few years, concern has been raised regarding the possibility of adverse reactions as a result of immunization with multivalent vaccines. There has been a call for vaccines covering just one disease (monovalent) since some people are convinced that it is multivalency that overloads the immune system and results in problems.

I have been in canine practice since virtually the birth of modern vaccination programs (more than 40 years) and can honestly say that I have not experienced major problems with multivalent products, although I have been concerned regarding the necessity of booster shots for each separate disease every year. My theory was, having experienced the scourge of distemper, parvovirus, and hepatitis, to name but three, if revaccination of them carried little risk and a lot of benefits, it should be advocated, and this I have done and continue to do with my own dogs.

Now, however, manufacturers are beginning to reintroduce single-component canine vaccines for those who wish to use them. I have to say that, with some of the more nervous breeds, vaccination using separate components, involving several spaced-out injections, results in considerably more stress and trauma to the dog than ever happened with, say, two shots a couple of weeks apart.

Vaccine manufacturers are also looking at the duration of immunity. Now, manufacturers are recommending annual checkups and spacing of the booster shots. Parvovirus is generally recommended annually. Distemper and hepatitis booster shots are recommended with some products, not annually, as in the past, but every

A dog's vaccination program should be tailored to the prevalence of disease in the area, and the dog's age and lifestyle.

two years. Since these recommendations now depend upon the particular product, it is wise to discuss not only the primary vaccination schedule but also the booster schedule very carefully with your veterinarian at the outset.

One undeniable fact that has emerged from the vaccination debate of the last few years is that now each dog's vaccination schedule is individually tailored to the particular circumstances. These include how much disease there is in the area, age, and lifestyle (for example, do you regularly go to shows or training classes, or board your dog?). All these factors are taken into account.

In the United States, annual vaccination is recommended. However, for adults, tests are recommended first to assess the dog's need for a booster shot.

As well as protecting your dog against potentially fatal diseases, vaccinations are essential if you intend to travel with your Beagle. When planning a trip, plan for your dog as well. Learn all the health rules in force regarding dogs in and to your destination, have your dog vaccinated in advance of your departure, and be sure to have that health certificate where you can reach it when requested.

Core vaccines

Core vaccines are those that protect against diseases that are serious, fatal, or difficult to treat. In the UK, these include distemper, parvovirus, and adenovirus (hepatitis). In North America, rabies is also included. For Beagle owners planning to travel with their dogs, protection is essential. They need to know what diseases are prevalent at their destination and see a veterinarian so the dog is vaccinated in time for immunity to take hold.

Noncore vaccines

Noncore vaccines are those against less serious diseases or those for which there is a special need. They include:

• Bordetella (kennel cough)

• Leptospira (kidney disease)

• Coronavirus (which causes diarrhea, especially in puppies)

• Borellia (Lyme disease, a tick-borne disease. A vaccine is available in North America but it is not currently licensed in the UK. The vaccine is known to cause reactions in a number of dogs.)

• Canine Herpes Virus (CHV) vaccine has recently been licensed in Britain. CHV is a major cause of so-called "fading puppy syndrome."

Canine distemper

As the result of vaccination, this once universal canine killer is now relatively rare in developed Western countries. Symptoms include fever, diarrhea, coughing, and purulent (pus) discharges from the nose and eyes. Sometimes the pads harden, a sign of the so-called "hardpad" variant. Further signs include skin pustules, respiratory symptoms, seizures and other neurologic signs, and muscle twitching.

Hepatitis

Canine hepatitis is more correctly called canine adenovirus 1 (CAV1) disease. Signs range from sudden death to mild cases where the dog appears to be only a little under the weather. Symptoms include fever, enlargement of the lymph nodes (glands), and a swollen liver. During recovery, "blue eye" can occur due to the swelling of the cornea (the clear part in front of the eye). Symptoms usually resolve very quickly without impairing the sight.

Rabies

This is an extremely serious zoonotic disease (meaning it is communicable to man). It is found on all continents, except Australasia and Antarctica. Some countries, including the UK, are considered free of the disease, often due to geographical barriers.

The virus is spread through bites from infected animals, particularly foxes in Europe; bats, foxes, racoons, and skunks in North America; and stray dogs in other parts of the world. Vaccination is mandatory in many countries, including the United States. In Britain, although rabies vaccines are now available, they are mandatory only if owners wish to travel with their dogs to certain authorized countries and return to the UK without undergoing the six months' quarantine.

Vaccination against rabies is mandatory in the United States.

Parvovirus

Canine parvovirus (CPV) is a relatively new disease, first recognized in 1978. In the 1980s, it caused problems worldwide. The main symptoms are vomiting and diarrhea containing blood. The control of this disease involved the rapid development of highly effective vaccines, which is one of the triumphs of modern veterinary medicine. However, it is still a major killer in many parts of the world, rivaling only that of distemper.

Leptospirosis

The leptospirosis component of multivalent vaccines is unique in that leptospiral organisms are bacteria and not viruses.

Two types are important in dogs, *L. canicola*, which is mainly transmitted in the urine of infected dogs, and *L. icterohemorrhagiae,* for which rats are the main vectors. Leptospirosis is communicable to humans. Country dogs can be at risk from infected waterways, particularly in areas that are heavily rat-infested. City dogs are infected from sniffing other dogs' urine.

L. icterohemorrhagiae spread by rats is by far the most devastating to the dog. It usually results in jaundice (icterus), which is a yellow coloration of the membranes and the skin. It is often first noticed when the white of the eye appears yellow. Death from liver and/or kidney failure can rapidly follow. One advantage is that, being caused by bacteria, leptospirosis, unlike the viral diseases, such as parvovirus, does respond to treatment using antibiotics. Nevertheless, vaccination is by far the wisest course, with regular booster shots according to your veterinarian's recommendations.

Parainfluenza

Parainfluenza virus is considered to be a primary causal agent in kennel cough syndrome (infectious bronchotracheitis) in North America. In the UK, the bacterium *Bordetella bronchiseptica* is considered to be the main cause. Yearly revaccination is advised by the manufacturers, with the suggestion that if your dog is going into high-risk situations, such as boarding kennels, even earlier revaccination should be considered.

Bordetellosis, tracheobronchitis, or kennel cough can spread like wildfire when dogs are closely congregated. Most Beagles are kept as pets today, but some are kept in small Beagle packs, and this is just the ideal situation for the spread of kennel cough (so too are boarding kennels). At certain times of the year, particularly when the weather is hot and humid, the infection can spread rapidly from dog to dog through coughing. If infected and susceptible, your Beagle can have a dry, hacking cough for three weeks or more. If healthy, there are usually no other signs.

Young puppies and very elderly dogs are at greater risk, particularly since recently it has been found that there are some virulent strains of Bordetella that cause serious disease, with the rapid onset of bronchopneumonia.

Vaccine in the form of nasal drops is particularly effective since it will give a workable immunity in 72 hours. Like the immune response to the natural disease, protection is relatively short-lived; therefore, dogs that are exposed to special risks should be revaccinated according to your veterinarian's recommendations, usually every six to ten months.

There is also a multivalent kennel cough vaccine available that incorporates Bordetella and parainfluenza.

Coronavirus

Canine coronavirus enteritis can cause diarrhea. It occurs most often in puppies. The disease is usually mild and responds well to supportive therapy. The virus can be shed in the feces for up to three weeks after apparent recovery. A vaccine is available in North America and some parts of Europe. There is currently no licensed vaccine available in Britain.

Borreliosis (Lyme disease)

This bacterial disease is carried by certain ticks whose bite can transmit the disease to dogs and to people. Common in parts of North America, it is now being increasingly diagnosed in the United Kingdom, particularly in southern England. It causes acute polyarthritis in both dogs and people. Sometimes, fever, heart, kidney, and neurological problems can occur.

Canine herpes virus

The recently introduced vaccine is very useful if you are breeding and have had problems with "fading puppies." The fading puppy syndrome can be caused by many factors, including

Young puppies are more vulnerable to parainfluenza.

bacterial and viral infections, poor husbandry, poor hygiene, etc. On both sides of the Atlantic, one of the main causes has been found to be canine herpes virus (CHV). It can cause the death of puppies in utero, resulting in much smaller litter sizes and also death of puppies within the first 14 days of life. Vaccination of the female just before or shortly after mating, followed by another vaccine just prior to whelping, has been shown to reduce neonatal mortality considerably. The immune response is relatively short-lived and revaccination has to be carried out with each litter.

PARASITE CONTROL

In planning preventive strategies for your Beagle, do not overlook parasite control. It is necessary to eliminate ectoparasites living on the outside of the body (fleas, lice, ticks, and mites), and also the "insiders" or endoparasites,

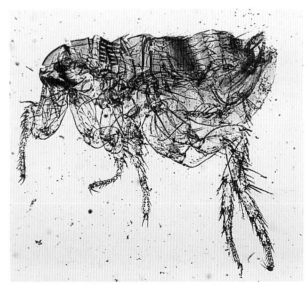

The dog flea—Ctenocephalides canis.

particularly roundworms and tapeworms, although others—microscopic protozoa such as *Coccidia* and *Giardia*—can cause bowel problems in certain areas, particularly in North America.

ECTOPARASITES
Fleas

These are the most common ectoparasite found on dogs. Some dogs will carry very high flea burdens without showing any signs, whereas others develop a flea allergy dermatitis (FAD) after only two or three flea bites. FAD is primarily an allergic response and some Beagles do have a reputation for allergies.

Flea control is important; fleas are not host-specific. Both dog and cat fleas can be found on dogs, cats, and humans. They can be picked up just as easily in backyards as they can in the country, since rabbits, squirrels, and raccoons can all carry them. A meal of blood is essential for the flea to complete its life cycle, and when the need arises, the opportunistic flea is just as likely to feed from us as from our pets.

Although the eggs may be laid on the dog, these drop to the ground. Provided the temperature and humidity are within the correct range, they soon develop into larvae (immature forms) in your carpets and the gaps between floorboards, or outside in areas where the temperature and humidity are fairly high.

For any flea control to be effective, both the adult fleas on your dog, and immature stages developing in the home, have to be controlled. Fleas developing outdoors are not so easily controlled, but routine flea treatment of your Beagle will prevent any adult fleas from being brought in to reinfect the home. Adult fleas account for only approximately 5 percent of the total flea population.

Once the female flea has attained the requisite blood meal, she commences egg laying. Although often occurring on the dog, supplied with the right conditions, the female may lay her eggs in the environment. The life cycle can be as short as three weeks. In suitable environments, adult fleas can survive for more than a year without feeding. This is the reason why pets and people are sometimes bitten when entering empty properties previously occupied by pets.

Control of the 95 percent of fleas in their immature stages can be much more difficult than the adult flea. In the home, thorough cleaning and vacuuming does much to remove the almost invisible immature stages. Although more larvicidal insecticides are coming on the market, most environmental sprays are effective mainly against adult fleas. Therefore, make sure that the insecticide you choose has prolonged action so that any newly matured adults are also killed.

Flea treatments

Your dog must also receive regular treatment. This can take several forms:

• Oral medication to prevent completion of the life cycle of the flea
• Applications in the forms of sprays, spot-on preparations, or powders
• Insecticidal baths.

Spot-on treatment has proved to be very effective against fleas and ticks.

Bathing is usually the first thing people think of when they find that their dog has fleas. If carried out effectively, insecticidal baths will kill any adult fleas on the dog, but they have very little residual effect, so it should be combined with some other method of flea control.

Spot-on preparations are very popular since they avoid the hissing noise of a spray, which upsets many dogs. They depend upon the use of sophisticated technology, which disperses the preparation over the invisible fat layer that covers the skin. The chemical does not actually enter the body, but, within 24 hours, will provide whole-body protection so that when the flea bites to obtain that all-essential blood meal, the mouth parts have to penetrate through the fat layer and consequently, the chemical is ingested.

Most spot-on preparations will give protection for up to two months and will survive two or three routine baths. Some spot-on preparations today not only prevent fleas but will also prevent infection with heartworm (*Dirofilaria*) and the most common form of roundworm (*Toxacara canis*). Collars and tags are also available containing slow-release products.

Very effective flea preparations are available over the counter from pet stores and supermarkets. Some Beagles have sensitive skins and may have allergic reactions (hypersensitivity), so it is worthwhile discussing the choice of product with your veterinarian. Many of the longer-lasting effective compounds are available from veterinarians only. Also, your veterinarian will be aware of the magnitude of the local flea problem and will therefore be able to advise you on an effective control strategy.

Lice

Lice are less common than fleas but are frequently seen in poorly reared puppies, such as those found in puppy farms (mills). Lice do not survive away from the host and therefore require direct contact for transmission. The eggs (nits) are attached to individual hairs (usually around the head and ears) and can be seen with the naked eye. Infestation is associated with intense irritation. Bathing is effective, using an ectoparasiticidal (flea) shampoo, but do not forget to wash or spray the bedding with an appropriate product.

Ticks

Ticks appear as small gray, brown, or whitish "warts" attached to the skin. Sheep and deer (and hedgehogs in the UK) are usually the primary hosts.

Ticks can be carriers of various diseases (such as Lyme disease, Babesiosis, and Ehrlichiosis). Many flea and louse preparations, including some spot-on preparations, are also licensed for tick control. The latter are particularly useful, since they retain their activity even if you bathe your Beagle between applications.

Harvest mites (chiggers)

These are parasitic immature forms (larvae) of a mite known as *Trombicula (Eutrombicula) alfreddugesi* (North American chigger). Colored orange-red, they live freely in organic matter and are just visible to the naked eye. Beagles are prone to harvest mite infestation, particularly if exercised in fields or woodland on a chalky subsoil in the fall. The feet and muzzle are most frequently affected. They cause intense irritation, which can often result in secondary infections that may be quite difficult to clear up.

Prolonged-action insecticidal sprays are effective. Also, change the exercise areas, particularly in the fall when the free-living adult mites are most active. This is especially important if your Beagle happens to have any inherent allergic skin problems.

Cheyletiella

This is a surface-living mite, which can just be seen with the naked eye. It can be a problem in

Beagle puppies, particularly if they have been reared in a rural location. The affected puppy will be itchy along the back and sometimes around the underparts. It is also known as "walking dandruff," although it isn't actually dandruff that you can see moving but a small, scalelike white mite. The mite is zoonotic (communicable to us) and can cause intense irritation in children. Symptomless adult dogs (carriers) are usually the source of infection in kennels. Treatment with any of the ectoparasiticidal preparations results in rapid cure.

Mange

This is a parasitic skin disease caused by mites that are invisible to the naked eye. Two types most commonly cause problems in dogs: demodectic mites and sarcoptic mites.

The demodectic mite lives in the hair follicles and generally causes no problems. However, if the dog's immune system is compromised for any reason, then the mites can multiply and mange results. They can cause hair loss around the face and eyes. This is seldom itchy but the areas can become infected, resulting in pyoderma (skin infection). Demodectic mange is not especially contagious. Effective remedies are available but since it is likely that there is an underlying immune-mediated problem, get veterinary advice. Treatment can be long and costly, if the condition becomes severe and widespread on the body.

By contrast, sarcoptic mange causes intense itching and is highly contagious, not only to dogs but to humans (scabies). It is an increasing problem, particularly with outdoor dogs such as

Beagles. Limbs, elbows, and ankles (hocks) are the main areas affected.

Diagnosis, as with demodectic mange, depends on identification of the causal mite under the microscope. Often, several skin scrapings have to be taken before there is a positive diagnosis. Treatment involves medication, shampoos, and other preparations prescribed by your veterinarian.

ENDOPARASITES
Roundworms

These are the most important internal parasites that affect dogs. Other endoparasites, such as *Giardia* and *Coccidia*, can cause chronic diarrhea and lack of growth in puppies, and are occasionally a problem (particularly in large kennels).

The common roundworm, *Toxacara canis*, measures 3 to 6 inches (7–15 cm). Puppies can be born with roundworms acquired from their mother before birth, due to the complicated life cycle of the worm. This is one of the reasons why roundworm infestation is so common.

The life cycle includes migration through the tissues of the host. Larvae (immature worms) can remain dormant in the tissues for long periods. Under the influence of hormones during pregnancy, they are activated, cross the placenta, and enter the puppy, where they develop into adult worms in the small intestine in a few days. At only 10 to 12 days old, puppies can shed infective roundworm eggs. Eggs are also passed from the female to the puppy via the milk during suckling.

Children can become infected (although it is not common), but the contagion can be prevented with good hygiene (hand washing after contact with the dog). It is also worthwhile consulting your veterinarian in order to formulate a comprehensive deworming plan, particularly if you have young children.

Often, infestation goes unnoticed, but if there is a heavy worm burden, the puppy will grow poorly and may have recurrent diarrhea and vomiting, together with a bloated appearance. Sometimes, live worms are passed and occasionally, obstruction of the bowel and death can occur. Adult dogs can carry heavy worm burdens and show virtually no signs. These dogs are a source of potential infection to others, since the microscopic eggs are passed through their stool.

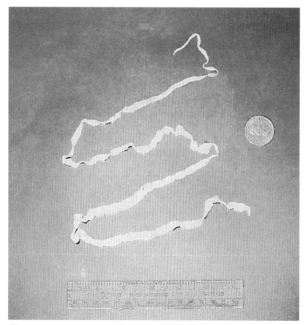

Tapeworm passed by an adult dog. (The coin gives an indication of size.)

Other parasitic worms

Other worms affecting the bowel include hookworm, *Ancylostoma*, and whipworm, *Trichuris*. These can be a problem in kennel dogs that have grass runs. Modern multiwormers usually contain components to combat these species. The canine lungworm, *Filarides osleri*, most commonly affects puppies and young dogs. The worm lives in nodules in the air passages and can cause coughing and loss of condition. Remedies are available from your veterinarian.

Tapeworms

Also known as cestodes, these are the other major class of common canine worms. Unlike roundworms, they need an intermediate host to complete their life cycle, so they cannot spread directly from dog to dog. *Dipylidium caninum* is the most common tapeworm of the dog and uses the flea as an intermediate host. Adult worms measure up to 20 inches (50 cm) and live in the intestine.

Although the eggs are invisible, the individual tapeworm segments (similar in size to a grain of rice) are shed from the end of the tapeworm as they mature and are passed through the stool. Sometimes, mature segments can be seen wriggling out of the anus. These are packed with eggs. Although unpleasant to see, tapeworm infestation usually has few effects on a normal healthy Beagle; in puppies, weight loss and poor condition can result.

Immature fleas (larvae) living in the environment swallow the microscopic tapeworm eggs, which develop as the flea matures. The adult flea is then swallowed by the dog during routine grooming and so the life cycle of the tapeworm is completed.

Effective tapeworm treatments are available, but fleas must also be controlled, so it is worthwhile consulting a veterinarian.

Heartworm

Dirofilaria immitis are large worms, up to 11.5 inches (30 cm). They cause serious problems because they mainly inhabit the right auricle (atrium) of the heart and the pulmonary artery. The parasite is transmitted by certain types of mosquito. It is prevalent in many parts of the United States and southern Europe. It has also been reported in Britain in imported dogs or dogs that have traveled under the PETS scheme to areas where heartworm is prevalent and then have reentered Britain without having undergone quarantine. Effective prophylactic measures to prevent infection, in the form of a once-a-month tablet, are available from veterinarians.

The Beagle is a lively dog, and it is all too easy for accidents to happen.

DEALING WITH EMERGENCIES

Beagles are amiable, active extroverts. Unfortunately, their inquisitive nature can often lead to the unexpected. Be prepared!

FIRST AID

First aid is the initial treatment given in any emergency. The purpose is to preserve life, reduce pain and discomfort, and minimize the risk of permanent disability or disfigurement.

First aid may be necessary as a result of seizures or collapse. Beagles love the great outdoors and it is not unknown for them to fall down holes, shafts, cliffs, etc. Regardless, of the emergency, there is often much that can be done via simple first aid.

I hope you will never have to use the following notes, but it is worthwhile being aware of what to do, just in case. They are basic principles that can act as your standby when faced with an emergency situation and can make the difference between life and death.

The responsible owner should have an understanding of the principles of first aid.

Priorities

- Keep calm and try not to panic.
- Get help, if possible.
- Contact the nearest veterinarian, explain the situation, and get first-aid advice.
- If there is possible injury, keep your dog as still as possible. With a dog the size of a Beagle, this can often be achieved by sitting with him in your arms. This also has the added advantage of providing him with warmth, which is essential if he is going into shock (see below). Try to cover him if you can.
- If there is a chance of broken bones, particularly if the spine is involved, lay the dog in a box (if possible) and cover him with a blanket.
- Shock is usually part of any emergency. For this, warmth can be lifesaving; therefore, wrap him in whatever is available—blankets, coats, even newspaper is better than nothing.
- Take your dog to the veterinarian as soon as possible.
- Drive carefully, observe speed limits, and, if possible, take someone with you, either to drive or to care for the dog while you drive.

Shock

Shock is a complex condition. Primarily due to lack of fluid in the cells, tissues, and organs of the body, it results in a serious drop in blood pressure. It can be caused by:

- Loss of blood volume due to bleeding
- Heart failure
- Acute allergic reactions
- Heatstroke (hyperthermia).

Signs of shock include:

- Rapid breathing and heart rate
- Pale mucous membranes of the gums, lips, or under the eyelids
- The feet or ears feel cold to the touch
- Vomiting may occur
- The dog may be uncharacteristically quiet and unresponsive.

First aid for shock should include:

- Conserving body heat (as above)
- Keeping the dog quiet and in dim light, if possible

- Seek immediate veterinary help, particularly if there is any bleeding (which you should attempt to control—see below)

The ABC of first aid

A   Airway
B   Breathing
C   Circulation (cardiac function)

Airway

If your Beagle has collapsed, is choking, or is bleeding profusely from the mouth, it is important to ensure that the airway is unobstructed in order to allow air (oxygen) to enter the lungs. Do your best to clear any obstructed airway, but take care. Do not put your hand in your Beagle's mouth. Remember, the dog is just as terrified as you are, and, if he is fighting for his breath, he may well bite in panic. Use any blunt object (such as a piece of wood) to open the mouth. Then use a tie or a piece of string looped over the teeth of the upper and lower jaws to open the mouth. With a piece of cloth wrapped around a stick or something similar, you can often clear any obstruction from the mouth. However, be careful not to push the object farther down the trachea.

Breathing

If your Beagle has collapsed and is not breathing, place him on his side with both forelegs pulled forward. With both hands, try gently pushing the chest just behind the elbow. At the same time, try to detect a heartbeat (pulse) at the same position. If no heartbeat can be detected, go swiftly to cardiac massage.

Cardiac function

In a normal, healthy nonobese Beagle, the cardiac pulse (heartbeat) can usually be seen or felt between the ribs on the left side, just behind the elbow, although this can sometimes be difficult with overweight dogs. Try feeling for the femoral pulse located on the inside of the thigh just above the knee joint where the femoral artery crosses the femur (thighbone).

Cardiac massage

Do not do this if there is a risk of chest injury. Go to mouth-to-nose resuscitation. If the dog is unconscious and you cannot detect a heartbeat, gently squeeze the ribs just behind the elbow approximately every one to two seconds. Check every minute or so to see if you can feel any movement below your fingers. If not, continue cardiac massage but also start mouth-to-nose resuscitation.

Mouth-to-nose resuscitation

- Pull the tongue forward and close the mouth.
- Place a handkerchief over the nose and mouth.
- Cup the hands around the handkerchief and blow forcibly to force air into the chest.
- Do this 10–20 times a minute.

FIRST-AID PROBLEMS
Hives ("nettle rash")

This is an acute allergic reaction or anaphylaxis. It is probably more important in Beagles than

Beagles tend to be more allergy prone than other breeds.

some other breeds because there is a breed predisposition to atopy, which is a particular type of allergic reaction. Some Beagles seem to be particularly allergy prone anyway.

Hives-type swellings can develop very quickly. They may be due to insect stings from bees, wasps, or hornets, or plant stings (true nettle rash). Foods or drugs in the form of oral medicines and injections (vaccines and antibiotics) can also be responsible.

It is very frightening if your dog's face suddenly swells to twice its normal size, but usually the swellings disappear quickly. Sometimes the swellings are extremely itchy (pruritic), and rubbing and scratching can make the condition worse. Bathe with cold water. Apply antihistamine cream if available and consult your veterinarian as soon as possible. An antihistamine injection is usually required, sometimes together with an anti-inflammatory.

Bleeding

With their love of exercise in rough terrain, Beagles probably suffer more than most with torn nails and cut feet. Torn nails are extremely painful, and, like footpads, bleed profusely. A firm bandage can be improvised from any reasonably clean material or even a plastic bag secured firmly over the paw. If a tight bandage has been applied, never leave it on for more than 15 minutes. The aim is to prevent blood loss. Get your pet to the veterinarian as soon as possible. If your Beagle resents having his foot touched, improvise a muzzle, using a piece of bandage, rope, or even a necktie. Attach it around his jaws and then behind the head just to take his mind off what is happening to his foot.

If there is hemorrhaging from an area where bandaging is impractical (for example, a bite wound to the throat or lips), try to control the bleeding by applying finger or hand pressure, preferably with a piece of clean bandaging material soaked in cold water between your hand and the wound.

Burns and scalds

Cool the burned area with cold water as quickly as possible.

• If the affected area is extensive, use wet towels.

- If the injury is due to a caustic substance, wash away as much of this as you can with plenty of cold water.
- Do not allow the dog to lick the substance or burned areas, or it will injure the mouth, esophagus, and stomach.
- If the burn is in the mouth, press cloths soaked in clean cold water between the jaws. Arrange to visit the veterinarian as soon as practicable.

Eye injuries

Foreign bodies, usually grass awns, or scratches from bushes, or even cats' claws, are not uncommon problems affecting the Beagle's eye. When exercising, all you usually see is the dog return with the affected eye tightly closed. He is likely to resent you handling the eye area.

- Try to muzzle, as above.
- If you cannot easily see the cause of the problem, cover the eye with a pad soaked in cold water or, better still, saline solution, such as contact lens solution.
- Keep the dog in subdued light, if possible.
- Seek veterinary help without delay.

It is important to prevent further injury to the eye, since most Beagles will rub the closed eye along the floor or paw at it frantically. Frequently the cause is a grass awn lodged under the lids. Often, part of the grass can be seen. If it can be removed easily, take it out. Even if the dog then seems to be okay, a veterinary checkup is worthwhile.

In the summer, grass awns can get into eyes, causing major problems.

Seizures

Convulsions or seizures can occur in Beagles. They may be due to a bang on the head or other injury, or may occur spontaneously as a form of epilepsy (which also occurs in the breed). Although very frightening for the onlooker, remember that your Beagle is not conscious during the seizure. The less you handle him, the less stimulation he has and the greater the chance the problem will rapidly resolve. If possible, place him in a dark, confined area where he cannot cause himself more harm.

Most seizures last only a few seconds, although it may seem like hours. Wait until there is some recovery before going to the veterinarian, otherwise the trip itself may precipitate further episodes. If the seizure continues for more than three or four minutes, contact your veterinarian immediately and seek instructions.

Be careful not to get bitten during a seizure.

Heatstroke

Heatstroke is the all-too-frequent result of dogs being left in cars with too little ventilation in warm weather. The car does not need to be in direct sunlight to kill; poor ventilation is sufficient.

The body temperature rises rapidly and this can result in irreversible damage. Signs start with panting and obvious distress. Unconsciousness and coma will quickly follow. Try to reduce body temperature as quickly as possible:

- Open all the windows or put the air conditioning on full and at its lowest level.
- If ice is available, place it on the head, under the tail, and between the legs.
- Wrap the still-wet animal in damp towels and take him to the veterinarian as soon as you can.

The Beagle is a hardy dog, and suffers from few breed-specific problems.

BREED-ASSOCIATED CONDITIONS

Compared with other popular breeds, the Beagle is one of the world's hardiest dogs, and there are few breed-related problems. What follows should not be considered comprehensive but indicates some of the more common breed-related conditions that can be encountered.

ATOPIC DERMATITIS

Beagles seem to have more than their fair share of atopic dermatitis. It is a hypersensitivity reaction similar to hay fever in humans, due to inhaling allergens such as house dust mites, pollens, and human and animal dandruff. Affected animals have an inherent predisposition to form antibodies to the inhaled allergens.

Signs are intense itching, usually involving the face, paws, and underparts. It may be seasonal, due to pollens, or year-round if due to substances such as house dust.

Bearing in mind that a different sort of allergy can result from fleas (FAD), the condition needs careful diagnosis, so see your veterinarian as soon as possible.

BEAGLE PAIN SYNDROME

This is a type of acute pain syndrome, also known as meningitis. It is due to inflammation of the meninges (coverings of the brain). The dog appears stiff, and frequently the condition is confused with a slipped disk, which can also occur in these very active extroverts. Initially, the dog just appears to have a stiff neck, and sometimes it progresses to fever and seizures. This condition seems to run in families and may be immune-mediated. If your dog does appear to be in pain, particularly neck pain, consult your veterinarian without delay. Treatment involving analgesics and antiinflammatories, often combined with antibiotics, usually results in a prompt improvement, although the condition can recur.

EPILEPSY

Another form of meningitis can result in seizures, which can be recurrent. If you are at any time concerned that your Beagle may have had a slight seizure, do not ignore it—discuss it with your veterinarian.

EYE PROBLEMS
Primary glaucoma

In the Beagle, a condition known as primary open angle glaucoma (POAG) has been shown to be recessively inherited—both parents are carriers. They transmit the condition although they appear normal. "Glaucoma" indicates an increase in intraocular pressure. Without treatment this will rapidly lead to blindness. "Primary" indicates that there is no previous problem affecting the eye that could have resulted in an increase in pressure. "Open angle" refers to the area in the eye from which the intraocular fluid is removed. In a normal eye, fluid produced in the eye is filtered from the drainage angle into the blood at a rate equal to production. Therefore, intraocular pressure remains normal. In POAG, the drainage angle appears normal (unblocked) but intraocular pressure slowly increases since the rate at which it allows drainage slowly decreases. This leads to pressure on the optic nerve and ultimately blindness.

Corneal dystrophy

Some Beagles develop small white spots or opacities in the cornea (the clear part of the eye). These deposits of fat usually form by the time the dog is five years of age. They are generally nonprogressive once developed and are painless. They seldom interfere with vision unless they are very large.

Cherry eye

This is more accurately a prolapse of the nictitans (third eyelid) gland, which lies beneath the third eyelid. Sometimes the gland protrudes over the edge of the eyelid and appears as a pink fleshy mass. The gland is involved in tear production. Should your Beagle suddenly develop "cherry eye," see your veterinarian without delay. Provided the prolapse is recent, surgery will often prevent recurrence.

SUMMARY

Finally, it should be borne in mind that these conditions have only been mentioned because they are known to occur in Beagles, but this does not in any way imply that they are common conditions. My view, having had many Beagles as patients over the years, is that they are generally remarkably healthy, long-lived dogs.

With good care and management, your Beagle should live a long, healthy life.